THE CONRAN COOKBOOKS

STARTERS WITH STYLE

ARABELLA BOXER

CONRAN OCTOPUS

This paperback edition published in 1994 by
Conran Octopus Limited
37 Shelton Street
London WC2H 9HN

First published in 1986

Photographer Grant Symon
Editorial Consultant Caro Hobhouse
House Editor Susie Ward
Art Director Douglas Wilson
Art Editor Clive Hayball
Photographic Art Direction Valerie Wright Heneghan
Home Economist Berit Vinegrad
Photographic Stylist Sue Russell-Fell
Art Assistant Nina Thomas

ISBN 1 85029 637 5

The publishers would like to thank the following
for their assistance with photographic props:
Heal's, 196 Tottenham Court Road, London W1;
The Conran Shop, Fulham Road, London SW3;
Habitat Designs Limited

Title page: Vegetable Julienne Soup (page 11)

Typeset by SX Composing, Essex
Printed and bound in China

CONTENTS

INTRODUCTION

The first course has a special importance, in that it sets the tone for the whole meal. It is now that your guests are at their most appreciative, their taste buds keenest, and it is now that your table can be seen to its best advantage.

Entertaining is very much a reflection of personal style, and it is the starter that first indicates this. If the meal is to be an elegant one, the first course may be served already assembled on individual plates – best done with cold food – before the guests arrive. This style of starter is perhaps a little too redolent of restaurants for my taste, but it does make serving very much easier and avoids any last-minute panic or rush. For a more informal meal, and this is what I prefer, large dishes can be set simply on the table for guests to help themselves. This gives a sense of generosity, with the possibility of second helpings, and a feeling that one is at home among friends. I like to see soup served from a huge tureen, or a whole pâté placed uncut on the table, with a jar of homemade preserves, and a freshly baked loaf of bread, unsliced on a board. I enjoy having two or three dishes on the table, especially for the first course, for this encourages people to hand them around, to be sociable.

Sometimes there is not enough time to make even the simplest cooked dish. The answer is to buy the best produce your local supermarket or delicatessen has to offer. Rather than buying cooked dishes, I prefer to get smoked salmon or eel, potted shrimps or gulls' eggs during their brief season. Parma ham, bresaola, or coarse Italian salami are other possibilities. Smoked salmon and eel or potted shrimps need only lemon wedges, black pepper, and thin slices of brown bread and butter. Gulls' eggs should be served with celery salt and paprika and brown bread and butter. Parma ham is good alone, and delicious with fruit: with wedges of melon, ripe figs, or pears cut in quarters. Bresaola is good served with a mound of ricotta, or alone, while salami is best served plain, with good bread and butter. A perfectly ripe melon is always a treat, especially when served with limes.

I keep flower arrangements to a minimum, even for formal meals, as dishes inevitably have to be passed around the table, and space is always at a premium. Instead I often have a dish of fruit, carefully chosen to look good together.

The choice of wine, and the manner of serving it, also contributes to the sense of occasion. While a silver coaster, or even a decanter, may add to a formal meal when fine wines are to be served, they would be totally inappropriate for a simple meal, when a country wine would probably be my first choice. On this sort of occasion, I tend to put two or three opened bottles directly on the table, or have them well in evidence nearby, for once again this conveys a feeling of hospitality.

Striking first courses can be made even more impressive with the right serving dishes and batterie de cuisine. For an elegant meal, small soufflés, tarts and mousses look very appealing, but these can only be achieved by having the right equipment in the kitchen. It is sensible, and a good investment, to set about accumulating a range of small containers in various shapes, sizes and materials. Round ramekin dishes in ribbed white china are traditional and nicest for soufflés and baked eggs, while tiny flan rings and tartlet tins are invaluable for pastry dishes. For individual mousses and timbales, which are to be turned out for serving, I suggest acquiring dariole (or castle pudding) moulds, and oval oeufs en gelée moulds, in seamless aluminium. An individual rounded pudding basin shape, also in aluminium, is ideal for small fish puddings, like the Salmon Moulds with Dill Sauce on page 53. I find the most useful sizes range between 4 fl oz (120 ml) and 6 fl oz (170 ml). Loaf tins, meant for baking bread, are inexpensive to buy and useful for making pâtés and terrines, while shallow rectangular Swiss roll tins are essential for making roulades. A few good baking sheets are vital, as is a large roasting tin, to use as a bain-marie.

For placing on the table, I am particularly attached to two or three large round dishes, almost flat, with no rim, in plain white ovenproof china. I use these for serving large quiches, or a number of small tarts, for various hors d'oeuvres, vegetable salads, and sliced salami or prosciutto. Peasant soups like bortsch or minestrone look best served in large shallow bowls, while elegant soups like consommé or Crème Sènégale may be drunk from small two-handled cups, preferably in thin china.

The dishes in this book cover a fairly wide range; I have tried to include some old favourites – classic dishes like aiolli and fritto misto – as well as some more modern ones, like hot vegetable mousses served with contrasting sauces. In the case of the traditional dishes I sometimes like to introduce a new element: with cannelloni, for instance, I have chosen to make a light sauce of uncooked tomatoes to replace the usual ragu. Many of the recipes are new; some are well-loved old ones which I have brought into line with current thinking about healthy eating. In almost every case I have reduced the fat content by the use of low-fat substitutes for cream. There are a number of these on the market; the ones I like best are fromage blanc – or fromage frais, as it is sometimes called – quark and low-fat yoghurt, all available from supermarkets. For richer dishes, I like to use crème fraîche, with its subtle acidity, instead of double cream.

Many of the dishes in this book complement one another, and a whole meal can be made from them, without any so-called 'main course'. You may choose to serve three or four together for an informal spread, with a salad and cheese to follow. This may be convenient for those requiring last-minute attention. Alternatively, you can serve two dishes, one after the other, in slightly larger quantities than usual, for an enjoyable light meal that fits in with current feelings about healthy eating. There is no need to feel tied to the structure of the conventional three-course meal, even for a dinner party. It is up to you to decide what is appropriate for the occasion, and what your guests will enjoy.

It is interesting to reflect how much the manner of serving can alter the character of a dish. I am often reminded of Gertrude Stein's cook, who used to make an omelette when Picasso, whom she admired, was coming to dinner; for another, less-favoured, painter she would merely make scrambled eggs, saying 'it takes the same number of eggs, but shows less respect . . . .

Arabella Boxer

CHILLED AUBERGINE SOUP

Grilling the aubergines gives this soup a smoky flavour that is subtle and unusual. This soup is creamy coloured without being rich, but is best followed by a 'dry' dish, roast or grilled meat for instance, rather than one in a sauce.

──────── SERVES 6 ────────

2½ lb (1.1 kg) aubergines
1 pint (560 ml) good chicken stock, free from fat
½ pint (280 ml) plain yoghurt
5 tablespoons lemon juice
for the garnish
1 large tomato, skinned
1 tablespoon chopped chives

Heat the grill. Grill the aubergines for 25-30 minutes depending on size, turning them so that they cook evenly until they are soft in the centre when pierced with a skewer.

Leave the aubergines to cool, then cut them in half and scoop out the flesh, discarding the skin. Chop roughly, and put in a food processor or blender with the chicken stock. Process until smooth, then add the yoghurt and lemon juice and process again, until very smooth.

Turn into a bowl and chill for 2-3 hours.

To make the garnish, dice the tomato, discarding the seeds and pulpy interior.

To serve the soup, pour into chilled soup cups, divide the garnish and add a little diced tomato, with chopped chives sprinkled over it, in the centre of each one.

ICED TOMATO AND PEPPER SOUP

An unusual soup, at the same time tart and spicy, this is very refreshing in hot weather. If you are unfamiliar with the taste of fresh coriander, try a little in the soup to make sure you like it; otherwise use chives for the garnish. This is good served before a creamy dish of fish or chicken, or a chicken pie.

──────── SERVES 6 ────────

1½ lb (675 g) tomatoes
12 oz (340 g) green peppers
1 pint (560 ml) good chicken stock, free from fat
½ teaspoon ground cumin
2 tablespoons orange juice
2 teaspoons lime juice
1½ tablespoons chopped coriander, or chives

Skin the tomatoes, cut them in quarters, and put in a food processor.

Stick the peppers on long skewers and grill them, or lay them over a gas flame, turning frequently until the skin is blistered and charred evenly all over. Cool until they are cold enough to handle, then scrape away the skin, rinsing off the last bits under the cold tap. Cut the peppers in pieces, discarding the seeds, and add them to the tomatoes.

Process until reduced to a hash, then add the chicken stock and process again until the mixture is reduced to a rough purée. Turn into a bowl and stir in the cumin, orange and lime juice, and the chopped coriander, if used. Chill for 2-3 hours, or overnight; the soup should be very cold indeed.

Serve the soup in chilled cups, adding the chives, if used, sprinkled over the soup.

Left: Iced Tomato and Pepper Soup, top: Saffron Bread (page 77), right: Chilled Aubergine Soup.

Left: Pumpkin Soup (page 10), centre: Spinach and Scallop Soup, right: Game and Lentil Soup (page 10).

SPINACH AND SCALLOP SOUP

This is an unusual soup, a smooth purée of spinach with sliced mushrooms and scallops suspended within it. Shelled prawns, or small strips of Dover sole, may be substituted for the scallops. It is best followed by a plain meat dish, either roast or grilled.

―――――――――― SERVES 6 ――――――――――

12 oz (340 g) spinach
6 oz (170 g) small button mushrooms
1 oz (25 g) butter
3 tablespoons sunflower oil
8 oz (225 g) potatoes, sliced
1¾ pints (1 litre) hot light chicken stock
6 large scallops
4 tablespoons fromage frais, or ¼ pint (150 ml) single cream
salt and freshly ground black pepper
2 tablespoons lemon juice

Remove the spinach stalks and wash the leaves, then shake well, pat dry and tear into pieces. Remove the mushroom stalks and chop them; wipe the caps and set aside.

Heat the butter and half the oil in a heavy saucepan and cook the spinach leaves and mushroom stalks gently for 4-5 minutes, then add the potatoes and the stock, with salt and pepper to taste. Cover and simmer for 20 minutes, then remove from the heat and leave to cool for 5-10 minutes.

Meanwhile, slice the mushroom caps and fry them for a few moments in the remaining oil, just until they start to soften, then drain off the cooking juices and set aside. Steam the scallops for 3-4 minutes, depending on size. Slice each scallop into 3 round slices, leaving the coral tongues intact.

When the soup has cooled, purée it in a food processor or pass through a sieve. Stir in the fromage frais or cream. Return to the pan and reheat, adding salt, pepper and lemon juice to taste. Add the sliced mushrooms and scallops. Serve immediately in heated bowls.

9

GAME AND LENTIL SOUP

Illustrated on pages 8/9

A perfect soup for Boxing Day or New Year's Eve.

———————— SERVES 6 ————————

the remains of 2 cooked pheasants carcases and finely-chopped
meat
1 large onion
2 thin leeks
1 large carrot, quartered
2 stalks celery
3 stalks parsley
1 small bay leaf
salt and freshly ground black pepper
6 black peppercorns
8 oz (225 g) green or brown lentils
4 small carrots
3 tablespoons olive oil

Start a day in advance. Keep the chopped meat from the carcases in the refrigerator. Put the carcases into a large saucepan with the outer layer of onion and its skin, the green parts of the leeks, the quartered carrot and the tough ends of the celery. Add 3½ pints (2 litres) cold water, with the herbs, salt and peppercorns. Bring slowly to the boil, skimming once or twice, then simmer, covered, for 3 hours. Strain the stock and chill it.

Next day, soak the lentils in cold water for 3 hours. Chop the reserved onion and celery and slice the reserved white parts of the leeks and the small carrots. Heat the oil in a heavy saucepan and cook the onions and leeks gently for 5 minutes, then add the celery and carrots and cook for a further 5 minutes. Reheat the stock. Drain the lentils, add to the pan and stir for 3-4 minutes, then add the hot stock. Add salt and pepper and bring to the boil, the simmer gently, half covered, for 35-45 minutes until the lentils are soft.

When the soup is cooked, check the seasoning and add stock if necessary. Stir in the diced pheasant, cover and stand for 5-10 minutes before serving.

PUMPKIN SOUP

Illustrated on pages 8/9

This is a beautiful autumnal dish, golden in colour and warm in flavour. The flavour develops if the soup is made a day in advance and reheated. If you have the time, you can hollow out a whole pumpkin and use it as a soup tureen; the scooped-out flesh can be used for making a pumpkin risotto or gratin. The soup in its own tureen makes a splendid centrepiece for a bonfire party.

———————— SERVES 6 ————————

2 oz (50 g) butter
1 tablespoon sunflower oil
1 onion, finely chopped
1 teaspoon ground coriander
1 teaspoon ground cumin
8 oz (225 g) pumpkin (trimmed weight), cut into chunks
8 oz (225 g) celeriac (trimmed weight), cut into chunks
1½ pints (840 ml) hot chicken stock
salt and freshly ground black pepper
8 oz (225 g) tomatoes, skinned and chopped
for the garnish
3 tablespoons chopped parsley

Heat half the butter and all the oil in a saucepan and cook the onion until transparent. Add the spices and cook for 2-3 minutes, stirring. Add the pumpkin and celeriac and cook over a gentle heat, stirring, for 4-5 minutes. Add the stock, bring to the boil and simmer for 25 minutes, half covered, until the celeriac is soft. Add salt and pepper to taste.

Meanwhile, melt the remaining butter in a small frying pan and cook the tomatoes briefly (about 4 minutes), just until they begin to soften. Add them to the soup.

Allow the soup to cool slightly, then purée it briefly in a food processor, stopping before it is totally smooth, or push through a coarse food mill. Reheat and pour into a heated tureen or a pumpkin shell warmed through in the oven. Serve sprinkled with parsley.

CREME SENEGALE

Illustrated on pages 13

A speciality of the exclusive Knickerbocker Club in New York, this excellent chilled summer soup is also good served hot. As it is quite rich, it should be followed by a simple dish, preferably grilled or poached fish. It must be made with a good homemade chicken stock; I sometimes buy a chicken especially for this soup, using the dark meat for another dish.

───────── SERVES 6 ─────────

1 oz (25 g) butter
1½ teaspoons light curry powder
2 tablespoons plain flour
1½ pints (840 ml) hot strong chicken stock
juice of ½ lemon
¼ pint (150 ml) single cream
salt and freshly ground black pepper
4 oz (120 g) boneless chicken breast, cooked
for the garnish (optional)
a little cayenne pepper

Melt the butter in a heavy saucepan and add the curry powder. Stir for 1 minute over a gentle heat, then blend in the flour and stir for a further 2-3 minutes. Gradually add the stock and stir constantly until thickened. Simmer for 4-5 minutes, then add the lemon juice, cream, and salt and pepper to taste.

Stand the pan in a sink full of cold water and leave to cool, stirring frequently to prevent a skin from forming. Once the soup has cooled to room temperature, chill in the refrigerator for a few hours, or overnight.

Just before serving, cut the chicken breast into neat cubes. Pour the soup into chilled soup bowls, divide the chicken garnish among them and sprinkle with a little cayenne pepper.

VEGETABLE JULIENNE SOUP

Illustrated on page 13

A clear vegetable soup is the perfect start to a formal meal. You should start to make it a day ahead. Cheese Straws (page 76) add an elegant touch.

───────── SERVES 6 ─────────

1 duck or pheasant carcase, preferably raw
1½ lb (675 g) chicken joints
1 large onion, unskinned and coarsely chopped
2 carrots, coarsely chopped
2 leeks, coarsely chopped
2 stalks celery, coarsely chopped
3 stalks parsley
1 bay leaf
6 black peppercorns
salt and freshly ground black pepper
a little lemon juice
for the garnish
1 small carrot
1 small leek
1 small turnip
sprigs of chervil

Put the carcase and chicken joints into a large saucepan and pour in 2½ pints (1.5 litres) cold water to cover. Bring slowly to the boil, then reduce to a simmer and skim for a few minutes until the surface is clear.

Add the vegetables, herbs, peppercorns and a little salt. Return to the boil, skimming again if necessary, then simmer, half covered, for 3 hours. Strain into a bowl and leave overnight to cool.

Prepare the garnish. Cut the carrot and leek into 1½-in (3.5-cm) strips like very thin matchsticks. Cut the turnip into strips of much the same thickness.

Reheat the soup, adding salt and pepper as required, and lemon juice to taste. Strain a little of the soup into a small saucepan and bring to the boil. Drop in the garnish vegetables and cook for exactly 1 minute, then remove. Garnish and serve the soup in heated bowls.

BORTSCH, WITH PIROSHKIS

A steaming tureen of ruby-coloured bortsch makes a handsome first course, especially when accompanied by a dish of piroshkis, traditional Russian pastries. Both the soup and the pastry can be made in advance. A light dish, perhaps a fish salad, is all that is needed to follow.

SERVES 6-8

1 onion
3 medium beetroot, uncooked
1 carrot
1 small turnip
2 stalks celery
1½ oz (40 g) butter
2 tablespoons tomato purée
1 tablespoon sugar
1½ tablespoons red wine vinegar
2 pints (1.2 litres) duck, game or beef stock
8 oz (225 g) green cabbage, coarsely shredded
salt and freshly ground black pepper
for the piroshkis
6 oz (170 g) cream cheese
6 oz (170 g) butter
9 oz (250 g) plain flour, sifted
¾ teaspoon sugar
for the filling
12 oz (340 g) minced beef
1½ oz (40 g) chopped onion
2 hard-boiled eggs, chopped
2 oz (50 g) butter
salt and freshly ground black pepper
1 egg yolk
1 tablespoon milk
for serving
⅓ pint (220 ml) sour cream

To make the soup, cut the onion, 2 of the beetroot, the carrot, turnip and celery into strips like thick matchsticks. Melt the butter in a flameproof casserole and cook the vegetables gently in it for 5 minutes, stirring.

Stir in the tomato purée, sugar, vinegar and ¼ pint (150 ml) of the stock. Cover and simmer for 15 minutes, then add the cabbage, the remaining stock and salt and pepper. Cover and cook gently for 1 hour. Towards the end of the cooking time, coarsely grate the remaining beetroot and put in a pressure cooker with ½ pint (280 ml) water. Bring to the boil and cook under pressure for 10 minutes; set aside.

To make the pastry, blend the cheese and butter in a food processor, or in a bowl, using a wooden spoon. Add the flour and sugar and mix until thoroughly blended. Wrap in clingfilm and chill in the refrigerator for 45 minutes.

To make the filling, fry the minced beef, without extra fat, in a non-stick frying pan for 2 minutes, then add the onion and cook, stirring frequently, until the beef has lost all its pinkness. Turn the mixture into a sieve and leave for 5-10 minutes to drain.

Put the beef mixture and the chopped eggs into a food processor and process until well blended, then turn into a bowl. Stir in the melted butter, season with salt and pepper and leave to cool.

One hour before serving, heat the oven to 350°F (180°C, gas mark 4). Roll out the pastry ⅛ in (3 mm) thick and cut into 3-in (7.5-cm) circles. Brush the edges with water. Place 1 teaspoon of the filling in the centre of each, lift the sides around it, and pinch together to seal, as if making a small Cornish pasty. Mix the egg yolk with the milk and use to brush the piroshkis all over. Place on a greased baking sheet and bake for 12-15 minutes, until golden brown.

Meanwhile reheat the soup, stir in the grated beetroot and its juice, check the seasoning, and pour into a heated soup tureen. Serve the piroshkis as soon after baking as possible, accompanied by sour cream in a bowl.

Above: Crème Sènégale (page 11)

Above: Vegetable Julienne (page 11) with Cheese Straws (page 76).

Above: Bortsch with Piroshkis.

Above: Fish Soup with Rouille (page 14).

FISH SOUP WITH ROUILLE

Illustrated on page 13

Fish soup made with a variety of fish and served with croutons of French bread spread with rouille, a fiery sauce based on mayonnaise, is almost a meal in itself. Little is needed to follow: a salad would be ideal.

— SERVES 6-8 —

2 lb (900 g) mixed white fish such as conger eel, monkfish, cod, grey mullet, lemon sole or plaice, filleted and skinned, bones and trimmings reserved, then cut into 1-1½-in (2.5-4-cm) pieces
1 onion, halved
1 carrot, halved
1 stalk celery, halved
1 bay leaf
salt and freshly ground black pepper
2 tablespoons olive oil
1 leek, sliced
1 clove garlic, crushed
2 tomatoes, skinned and finely chopped
2 sprigs fennel
2-in (5-cm) strip orange peel
1 sachet powdered saffron
grated Parmesan or Grùyere cheese
for the rouille
4 cloves garlic, chopped
2 red chilli peppers
2 egg yolks
9 fl oz (250 ml) olive oil
1 sachet powdered saffron
for the garnish
1 stick dry French bread, thinly sliced

Put the fish bones and trimmings, onion, carrot and celery into a large saucepan. Pour in 2½ pints (1.5 litres) cold water to cover and add the bay leaf, salt and pepper. Bring to the boil slowly, skimming off any scum that rises to the surface, and boil gently, half covered, for 20 minutes. Strain and discard the bones and flavouring vegetables.

Heat the oven to 275°F (140°C, gas mark 1).

Put the sliced bread on a baking tray and leave it in the oven, turning once, until pale golden and very dry.

To make the rouille, reduce the garlic and chillies to a paste in a food processor, or in a mortar with a pestle. Transfer the paste to a bowl, add the egg yolks and beat with a wooden spoon until well blended. Gradually beat in the oil, at first drop by drop, then in a thin trickle, exactly as if making mayonnaise. When all the oil is absorbed, stir in the saffron. Set aside. (This may be made a day in advance and kept in the refrigerator, closely covered.)

To make the soup, heat the oil in a heavy saucepan and cook the sliced leek for 3 minutes. Add the garlic and tomatoes and cook for a further 2 minutes. Bury the fennel and orange peel among the vegetables. Lay the coarser fish (conger eel, monkfish, cod, etc.) on the vegetables, cover the pan, and cook gently for 3-4 minutes, then pour on the fish stock and bring to the boil. Boil steadily, quite fast, for 10 minutes, then lower the heat and add the softer fish. Simmer for a further 5 minutes, then turn off the heat and stir in the saffron. Leave to stand, covered, for 5 minutes.

Spread some of the croutons with rouille, allowing 2-3 for each person. Serve the soup either in heated individual soup plates with one or two croutons floating in each, or in a heated tureen accompanied by the croutons on a serving plate. Serve the remaining rouille in a bowl with the remaining croutons handed separately, and pass the Parmesan or Gruyère in another bowl, to be sprinkled on top of the floating rouille-coated croutons.

CANNELLONI

Illustrated on page 18

Fresh pasta is readily available nowadays, and lasagne sheets can be cut and used to make cannelloni. This dish involves quite a lot of work, even with bought pasta, but it looks splendid, and is so good and filling that it needs little to follow. It may also be prepared, partly or wholly, in advance, and baked only at the last moment. It can also be frozen, but thaw to room temperature before baking, or you may crack your dish.

─────────── SERVES 6 ───────────

6 sheets fresh lasagne, green if possible
1 tablespoon vegetable oil
for the filling
1 lb (450 g) spinach leaves
salt and freshly ground black pepper
2 tablespoons sunflower oil
2 oz (50 g) large spring onions (trimmed weight) bulbs only, sliced
8 oz (225 g) mushrooms, caps only, chopped
8 oz (225 g) ricotta cheese
for the tomato sauce
2 tablespoons sunflower oil
½ bunch spring onions, bulbs and young green leaves, sliced
1 lb (450 g) tomatoes, skinned and chopped
for the cream sauce
2 oz (50 g) butter
3 tablespoons plain flour
½ pint (280 ml) hot chicken stock, homemade if possible
¼ pint (150 ml) single cream
salt and freshly ground black pepper
4 tablespoons freshly grated Parmesan cheese
for the garnish
3 tablespoons freshly grated Parmesan cheese
sprigs of flat-leaved parsley

Cut the lasagne sheets in half. Bring a wide saucepan of water to the boil and cook the lasagne, 4-5 pieces at a time, for 2-6 minutes until tender. Lift the lasagne out and drop into a large bowl of cold water with the oil added. Allow to cool, then drain on a cloth. Cook the remaining lasagne in the same way.

To make the filling, cook the spinach in lightly salted boiling water for 4-5 minutes, then drain in a colander. When cool enough to handle, squeeze out all the moisture, then chop finely on a board or in a food processor. Set aside.

Heat the oil in a frying pan and cook the spring onions for 2-3 minutes, then add the mushrooms. Cook, stirring, until softened, then add the spinach and mix well. Remove from the heat and add the ricotta, mashing it into the vegetables with the back of a wooden spoon. Add salt and pepper to taste, and set aside.

To make the tomato sauce, heat half the oil in a frying pan and fry the spring onions gently for 2 minutes. Remove with a slotted spoon and place with the tomatoes and remaining oil in a food processor or coarse food mill. Process until roughly chopped, and set aside.

Grease a large rectangular dish with oil. Put 2 tablespoons of the filling on each piece of lasagne and roll up from one short end. Lay the rolls side by side in the dish and spoon the tomato sauce over them. Set aside.

One hour before serving, heat the oven to 375°F (130°C, gas mark 5).

To make the cream sauce, melt the butter in a saucepan, blend in the flour and cook for 1 minute, stirring. Gradually add the stock, stirring until blended. Simmer for 3 minutes, then add the cream, and salt and pepper to taste. Cook for 1 minute, then add the Parmesan cheese and stir until melted. Pour the sauce over the cannelloni without covering them completely; the tomato sauce and green pasta should show through here and there. Sprinkle with grated Parmesan and bake for 35 minutes, until golden brown. Serve hot, decorated with sprigs of Italian flat-leaved parsley.

CHICKEN LIVER PILAF

This dish is quite quick and simple to make. It would go nicely before a fish dish, or a vegetable casserole.

───────── SERVES 6 ─────────

1 lb (450 g) chicken livers
2 oz (50 g) butter
2 tablespoons olive oil
2 cloves garlic, finely chopped
3 tablespoons pine kernels
3 tablespoons currants
1 teaspoon ground allspice
1 lb (450 g) risotto rice
2 pints (1.2 litres) hot chicken stock
salt and freshly ground black pepper
2 tablespoons chopped parsley
for the accompaniment
4 pitta breads
1½-2 oz (40-50 g) butter

Heat the oven to 400°F (200°C, gas mark 6). Trim the chicken livers, discarding any discoloured parts, and chop roughly. Heat the butter and oil in a frying pan and fry the garlic for 1 minute, stirring, then add the livers. Stir over a fairly high heat for 3 minutes, until they have lost their pinkness, then remove with a slotted spoon and keep warm in a covered dish.

Add the pine kernels, currants, allspice and rice to the pan. Stir for a few minutes over a moderate heat, then add the stock. Cover and simmer for 15-18 minutes, until the rice is cooked and the stock absorbed.

Meanwhile, warm the pitta breads briefly in the oven (just long enough to soften), then split in two and spread lightly with butter. Place on a baking sheet and return to the oven for 6-8 minutes, until crisp and golden brown. Keep warm in a covered dish until the rice is done.

Stir the chicken livers into the cooked rice and add salt and pepper to taste. Reheat gently for a few moments, then turn into a heated serving dish, sprinkle with parsley and serve, accompanied by the hot pitta.

GREEN RISOTTO

This pretty dish is a speciality of the eighteenth-century restaurant, Del Cambio, in Turin. Like all very simple dishes, it must be made with the finest ingredients: the freshest spinach, the best arborio rice, homemade chicken stock, good olive oil and freshly grated Parmesan.

───────── SERVES 6 ─────────

7-8 oz (200-225 g) fresh spinach
1½ oz (40 g) butter
1½ tablespoons olive oil
3 shallots, finely chopped
12 oz (340 g) arborio rice
1¾ pints (1 litre) hot chicken stock, homemade
salt and freshly ground black pepper
for serving
freshly grated Parmesan cheese

Put the spinach leaves into a juice extractor, to get about 6 tablespoons spinach juice.

Heat the butter and oil in a frying pan and cook the shallots for 3 minutes. Add the rice and stir for 2 minutes, then pour in ½ pint (280 ml) of the stock. Cook gently, stirring often, until the stock is almost absorbed.

Reheat the remaining stock and add ⅓ pint (200 ml) to the pan. Continue to cook over a moderate heat, until nearly all has been absorbed.

Reheat the remaining stock and add half of it to the rice. Cook until absorbed, by which time the rice should be almost tender. Stir in the spinach juice and cook for a few moments longer, just until absorbed. If the rice is not yet tender, add a little more stock and cook a little longer. Total cooking time should be almost exactly 15 minutes.

Season to taste with salt and pepper and turn into a heated shallow serving dish. Serve immediately, accompanied by a bowl of grated Parmesan cheese.

Left: Chicken Liver Pilaf, right: Green Risotto.

Left: Cannelloni (page 15), right: Mixed Fresh Noodles with Mushrooms.

MIXED FRESH NOODLES WITH MUSHROOMS

This dish is beautiful with golden girolles or other wild mushrooms, but it is also delicious made with field mushrooms. Make just before serving, and follow with a dish that can be prepared ahead, like vitello tonnato.

SERVES 6

---

8 oz (225 g) fresh egg noodles
8 oz (225 g) fresh wholewheat noodles
4 tablespoons olive oil
4 shallots, chopped
3 cloves garlic, finely chopped
12 oz (340 g) mushrooms, sliced
8 tablespoons chopped flat-leaved parsley
salt and freshly ground black pepper
a little light soy sauce

Bring 2 saucepans of lightly salted water to the boil.

Meanwhile, heat the oil in a heavy frying pan and fry the shallots for 2 minutes, then add the garlic and fry for 1 further minute. Add the mushrooms and cook, stirring frequently, until softened. Add the parsley, salt, pepper and soy sauce, stir well and remove from the heat.

Cook the noodles in separate pans of boiling water until just tender (al dente). (If the noodles are really fresh, this will take only 2-3 minutes.) Drain in two colanders and turn into a heated serving bowl. Add the mushrooms and toss to mix. Serve immediately.

GREEN GNOCCHI WITH TOMATO AND BASIL SAUCE

Illustrated on page 21

These little dumplings, made with eggs and flavoured with spinach and ricotta, are one of my favourite first courses. They may be served with a tomato and basil sauce, or simply with melted butter and grated Parmesan cheese. Serve a plain roast bird to follow.

SERVES 6

---

12 oz (340 g) cooked drained spinach (allow 1½ lb (675 g) uncooked)
1½ oz (40 g) butter
salt and freshly ground black pepper
freshly grated nutmeg
9 oz (250 g) ricotta
1½ oz (40 g) grated fontina or Parmesan cheese
3 eggs, beaten
4 tablespoons plain flour, sifted
for the tomato and basil sauce
1 oz (25 g) butter
1 small onion, finely chopped
14 oz (420 g) tinned chopped tomatoes
a pinch of sugar
2 tablespoons basil leaves, torn into strips

Start a day in advance. Squeeze out the excess moisture from the spinach and process in a blender or food processor to make a smooth purée. Put into a saucepan and stir over a gentle heat, to dry out. Stir in the butter and season with salt, pepper and nutmeg. Add the ricotta, mashing with a wooden spoon until thoroughly blended. Add the cheese and stir until melted.

Turn off the heat and stir in the eggs, then the flour. Turn the mixture into a shallow dish and leave to cool. Chill, uncovered, overnight in the refrigerator.

Next day, make the sauce. Melt the butter in a saucepan and cook the chopped onion gently for about 3 minutes, until it starts to colour. Then add the tomatoes with their juice and simmer gently for 10-12 minutes until thickened. Season with salt, pepper and sugar. Allow to cool for a few moments, then process briefly in a blender or food processor to make a slightly chunky, not smooth, purée. Return to the pan and set aside.

Shortly before serving, bring a wide saucepan of water to the boil. Using two large teaspoons, form the spinach mixture into oval egg shapes and lay them on >

<a lightly floured board. When the water boils, reduce heat to simmering point and gently lower in the gnocchi, just a few at a time, to give them plenty of room to cook. Poach them gently for 4-5 minutes, removing them with a slotted spoon as they float to the surface. Test one to make sure each batch is cooked, then drain briefly on a cloth, and transfer to a heated serving dish.

Meanwhile, gently reheat the sauce, stir in the basil and remove from the heat. Cover and leave to stand until all the gnocchi are cooked. Pour the sauce over them and serve immediately.

GREEN PANCAKES WITH TOMATO FILLING

Lay the pancakes in rows in a large serving dish or serve them in individual dishes. Follow with a fairly simple dish, perhaps a cold poached fish, with mayonnaise and a green salad.

SERVES 6

for the batter
2 bunches watercress (3 oz (85 g) trimmed weight)
6 fl oz (170 ml) milk
4 oz (120 g) plain flour
a pinch of salt
1 large egg
for the filling
1 lb (450 g) tomatoes, skinned and chopped
1 oz (25 g) butter
2 teaspoons plain flour
½ pint (150 ml) sour cream
salt and freshly ground black pepper
for the sauce
1½ oz (40 g) butter
2 tablespoons plain flour
½ pint (280 ml) hot, homemade chicken stock
¼ pint (150 ml) single cream
4 tablespoons freshly grated Parmesan cheese
to finish
3 tablespoons freshly grated Parmesan cheese

Make the batter 1 hour in advance. Wash the watercress well, then cook in water just to cover for 6 minutes. Transfer to a food processor, using a slotted spoon. Boil the liquid in the pan until reduced to 4 tablespoons, then add to the watercress. Process until reduced to a purée, then make up to a scant ½ pint (275 ml) with milk.

Sift the flour and salt into the food processor, add the egg and process. Add the watercress mixture through the lid while the machine is still running, until smoothly blended. Set aside to rest for 1 hour.

To make the filling, cook the tomatoes for 4-5 minutes in the butter in a heavy saucepan. Blend in the flour, then stir in the sour cream and salt and pepper to taste. Cook for 3 minutes, stirring constantly, then set aside and keep warm.

To make the sauce, melt the butter, blend in the flour and cook for 1 minute. Gradually stir in the stock, cream, grated Parmesan cheese and salt and pepper to taste. Stir until the cheese has melted. Set aside and keep warm.

To assemble the pancakes, process the batter once more, and pour into a jug. Heat a non-stick frying pan or crepe pan and melt a tiny piece of butter in it. Pour in about 2 tablespoons of the batter, and swirl around the pan until you have a pancake about 5 in (12.5 cm) in diameter. When lightly browned on the underside, turn and cook on the other side, then remove from the pan and fill, while cooking the remaining pancakes (there should be 12 in all) in the same way. Fill with the tomato mixture.

Arrange the filled pancakes in a large heated serving dish or in individual dishes and then reheat the sauce, beating it well, and dribble over the pancakes. Sprinkle with Parmesan cheese.

Keep in a warm oven 225°F (110°C, gas mark low) until ready to serve.

Left: Green Pancakes with Tomato Filling, right: Green Gnocchi with Tomato and Basil Sauce (page 19).

SHELLFISH AND PASTA SALAD

I don't usually like pasta salads, but this one is exceptional, based on a dish created by my friend and colleague Melanie de Blank. Almost any dish of meat, poultry or game would go well after this.

SERVES 6

12 oz (340 g) halibut, skin and bones removed
1 lb (450 g) unshelled cooked prawns, or ½ lb (225 g) peeled prawns
6 oz (170 g) smoked salmon, sliced fairly thickly
1 lb (450 g) thin noodles
6 tablespoons olive oil
2-3 tablespoons lemon juice
salt and freshly ground black pepper
2-3 tablespoons chopped chives or dill
2-3 tablespoons chopped flat-leaved parsley

Poach the halibut in lightly salted simmering water for about 10 minutes, or until cooked. Drain and leave to cool, then discard skin and bone and break up into flakes, cutting any very large flakes in half. Shell the prawns and cut the smoked salmon into thin 1-in (2.5-cm) strips.

Cook the noodles in a large saucepan of lightly salted boiling water until just tender (al dente). (If the noodles are really fresh, this will take only 2-3 minutes.)

Turn the noodles into a large bowl. Reserve a few pieces of halibut and smoked salmon and a few prawns for the garnish, and gently fold the remainder into the noodles.

Mix the oil and lemon juice in a small bowl and add salt and pepper to taste. Stir into the noodles, with the herbs, shortly before serving.

Turn into a serving dish and scatter the reserved fish over the top. Serve with Saffron Bread (page 77), Bread Sticks (page 78), or Melba Toast (page 54).

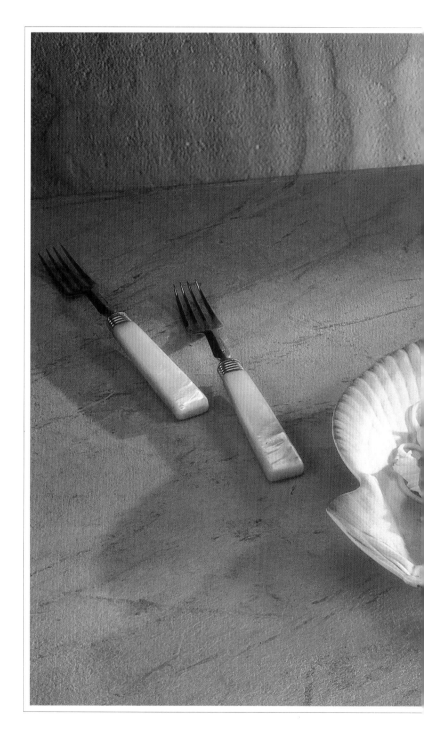

Below: Shellfish
and Pasta Salad.

AIOLLI GARNI

This vegetarian version of aiolli garni makes a good first course, while the classic dish, using either a whole boiled chicken or a large piece of fish, is more suitable for a main course. Little is needed to follow, perhaps a pasta dish, or a risotto.

———————— SERVES 6 ————————

12 oz (340 g) broccoli, or 1 small cauliflower
12 oz (340 g) French beans
12 oz (340 g) small new potatoes
8 oz (225 g) cherry tomatoes, or 6 small tomatoes
6 large eggs
salt and freshly ground black pepper
for the aiolli
3-4 large cloves garlic, peeled
2 large egg yolks
a pinch of salt
12 fl oz (350 ml) best olive oil
about 1 tablespoon white wine vinegar
about 1 tablespoon lemon juice

First make the aiolli: peel and chop the garlic cloves finely, then pound them to a hash in a mortar with a pestle, or push them through a garlic press into a heavy bowl, and pound with the back of a wooden spoon. Add the egg yolks one at a time, beating well until thoroughly blended with the garlic. Add the salt, then begin adding the olive oil, a few drops at a time, as if making mayonnaise. When the mixture begins to thicken, start adding the oil in a thin stream, stopping every few seconds but beating constantly. Continue until all the oil has been absorbed, then gradually add the vinegar and lemon juice, tasting as you do so.

Shortly before serving, cook the vegetables. Divide the broccoli into sprigs; trim the beans, leaving them whole. Scrub the potatoes, leaving the skins on. Cook the broccoli and the beans in separate pans or lightly salted boiling water, until very slightly underdone. Drain well. Cook the potatoes in boiling salted water until tender, then drain. Boil the eggs, drain and plunge briefly into cold water, then shell them and cut them in half lengthways.

To serve, arrange the warm cooked vegetables and eggs on a large platter. Accompany with the aiolli in a simple earthenware bowl.

BAKED POTATOES WITH CAVIAR

This is a good dish to make with lumpfish roe, or even with a small tin of caviar. The second version uses chopped anchovies and fromage blanc. Follow with something fairly light, perhaps a cold beef salad.

———————— SERVES 6 ————————

for version 1
3 baking potatoes
4 oz (120 g) black lumpfish roe or caviar
¼ pint (150 ml) sour cream
3 tablespoons very finely chopped chives or parsley
for version 2
3 baking potatoes
3½ oz (100 g) tinned anchovy fillets
¼ pint (150 ml) milk
8 oz (225 g) fromage blanc or quark
3 tablespoons very finely chopped chives or parsley

Heat the oven to 400°F (200°C, gas mark 6). Scrub the potatoes and pat dry. Prick in several places with a fork. Bake them for 1-1¼ hours, or until soft in the centre.

For version 1, cut each potato in half, and put a spoonful of lumpfish roe in the centre of each half. Top with a spoonful of sour cream. Sprinkle with chives and serve immediately on hot plates.

For version 2, rinse the anchovy fillets under cold running water and soak for 15 minutes in the milk. Rinse and pat dry. Chop quite finely and mix with the fromage blanc.

Cut each potato in half and put a spoonful of fromage blanc and anchovies in the centre of each. Sprinkle with chives and serve immediately on hot plates.

Clockwise from top: Aiolli Garni; Fennel in Cheese Sauce (page 27); Baked Potato with Caviar and Sour Cream.

Above: Mixed Stuffed Vegetables.

FENNEL IN CHEESE SAUCE

Illustrated on page 25

This is good before a cold main dish or a roast game bird. Warming and quite substantial, it may be prepared fully in advance, then reheated in a hot oven (400° F/ 200° gas mark 6) for 25-30 minutes instead of browning under the grill.

SERVES 6
---

6 medium bulbs fennel
salt
for the sauce
2 oz (50 g) butter
3 tablespoons plain flour
¾ pint (420 ml) hot chicken stock, homemade
¼ pint (150 ml) crème fraîche, fromage blanc or quark
salt and freshly ground black pepper
4 oz (20 g) Gruyère cheese, grated
freshly grated nutmeg
4 tablespoons freshly grated Parmesan cheese

Trim the fennel, reserving any green leaves for the garnish. Cook the bulbs gently in a large saucepan of lightly salted boiling water for 30-40 minutes, or until tender when pierced with a skewer.

Meanwhile, make the sauce: melt the butter in a saucepan, add the flour and cook for 1 minute, stirring. Gradually add the stock, stirring until blended. Simmer for 3 minutes, then add the crème fraîche and salt and pepper to taste. Stir in the Gruyère cheese and a little nutmeg. Continue to cook gently, stirring, until the cheese has melted and the sauce is smooth, then set aside. If using fromage blanc or quark, stir in after the cheese and seasonings have been added, and the sauce is smooth. Do not allow to boil again.

When the fennel are cooked, drain them in a colander, then cut them in half lengthways and lay them cut side down in an ovenproof serving dish. Pour the sauce over and sprinkle with the Parmesan cheese. Brown under a hot grill, and serve immediately.

MIXED STUFFED VEGETABLES

This makes a pretty dish to start a dinner party; for a simple meal, make any one of the three vegetables, but in double quantities. The choice of vegetables could also include hollowed out courgettes and slices of boiled beetroot. Serve them at room temperature.

SERVES 6
---

12 flat mushrooms
3-4 tablespoons olive oil
1 large aubergine
6 tomatoes
for the stuffing
1 yellow or red pepper
1 green pepper
1 lb (450 g) tomatoes, skinned and chopped
½ mild Spanish onion, chopped
3 stalks celery, chopped
1 large clove garlic
3 tablespoons olive oil
1½ tablespoons lemon juice
½ teaspoon coriander seeds
salt and freshly ground black pepper
half-quantity Guacamole (page 32)
for the garnish
a few rosettes of mâche or sprigs of watercress

Heat the oven to 350°F (180°C, gas mark 4). Wipe the mushrooms, remove the stalks and lay them gills uppermost on an oiled baking sheet. Brush them with olive oil and bake for 15 minutes. Leave to cool.

Cut the unpeeled aubergine into slices about ¼ in (5 mm) thick. Brush all over with oil. Grill for 4 minutes on each side, until golden-brown. Cool. Skin the tomatoes by dipping into boiling water, then peeling off the skins. Cut off the tops and hollow out the insides.

To make the pepper stuffing, grill the peppers, turning often, until the skins are charred and blistered evenly all over. Scrape away the skin and discard the seeds. Chop the flesh, keeping the yellow or red separate >

< from the green pepper flesh.

Mix the tomatoes, onion, celery and garlic in a large bowl. Stir in the olive oil, lemon juice, coriander and salt and pepper to taste. Divide the mixture equally between two bowls, and stir the yellow or red pepper into one and the green pepper into the other.

Shortly before serving, pile the yellow or red pepper stuffing on to the mushrooms, and the green pepper stuffing on to the aubergines. Fill the tomatoes with the guacamole. Arrange on a large platter, or on individual plates, decorated with mâche or sprigs of watercress.

FRITTO MISTO

This version of Italian fritto misto uses vegetables instead of fish. It must be made at the last moment, so choose something to follow that can be made ahead.

— SERVES 6 —

for the batter
4 oz (120 g) plain flour
a pinch of salt
2 tablespoons sunflower oil
6 fl oz (170 ml) tepid water
1 egg white
for the vegetables
1 aubergine
salt
3 large courgettes
2 beefsteak tomatoes
8 oz (225 g) broccoli
for the garlic sauce
½ pint (280 ml) plain yoghurt
2 cloves garlic, crushed
a pinch of salt
for deep-frying
1 pint (560 ml) corn oil
for the garnish
2 lemons (or limes), quartered or sliced
sprigs of parsley

The garlic sauce can be made well in advance. Beat the yoghurt until smooth, then stir in the garlic and salt. Cover and chill in the refrigerator.

Make the batter 1 hour in advance, if possible. Sift the flour with the salt into a large bowl. Make a well in the centre, add the oil and beat, gradually adding the water to make a smooth thick batter. (The batter may also be made in a food processor.) Cover and leave for 1 hour.

About 30 minutes before cooking, cut the aubergine into diagonal slices about ⅛-in (3-mm) thick. Place in a colander and sprinkle with salt. Leave to drain for 30 minutes, then rinse and dry in a cloth, squeezing out excess moisture. Cut the courgettes into diagonal slices, and slice the tomatoes vertically. Pat the courgettes and tomato slices in a cloth to remove any excess moisture. Divide the broccoli into florets.

Beat the batter well. Whisk the egg white stiffly and fold it in.

Heat the oil in a deep-fryer or wok to 360°F (180°C). Dip the aubergine slices into the batter, shaking off the excess, and deep-fry for about 2 minutes on each side, until puffed and golden brown. Lift out immediately and drain on kitchen paper. Keep warm.

Reheat the oil to 360°F (185°C). Dip the courgette slices in the batter, shake off the excess, deep-fry in the same way and keep warm with the aubergine slices. Dip the broccoli florets in the batter, and fry in the same way.

When all are cooked, arrange on a large platter and garnish with lemons or limes and the parsley. Serve immediately, accompanied by the garlic sauce in a separate bowl.

Top: Fritto Misto, below: Caponata (page 32).

SPINACH ROULADE

This is an elegant first course, ideal for a dinner party on a summer evening. It takes all your attention for the last 10 minutes, so choose something very simple to follow. A dish of chicken in aspic, or cold salmon, would be a good choice.

SERVES 6
---

for the filling
8 oz (225 g) ricotta, or curd cheese, or quark
2 tablespoons plain yoghurt
salt and freshly ground black pepper
2 tablespoons chopped spring onions
2 tablespoons chopped chervil, or tarragon, or parsley
for the tomato sauce
½ bunch spring onions, bulbs and young green leaves, sliced
2 tablespoons sunflower oil
1 lb (450 g) tomatoes, skinned and quartered
for the roulade
1½ lb (675 g) fresh spinach
3 tablespoons double cream
5 large eggs, separated
3 tablespoons grated Parmesan cheese

To make the filling, beat the ricotta until smooth, then stir in the yoghurt, adding salt and pepper to taste. Stir in the spring onions and the herbs. Set aside.

To make the sauce, cook the spring onions gently in half the oil for 2 minutes, then remove with a slotted spoon and put them into a food processor with the tomatoes and the remaining oil. Process briefly to make a slightly chunky, not smooth, purée. Pour into a small saucepan and set aside.

To make the roulade, heat the oven to 400°F (200°C, gas mark 6). Line a shallow 12×8-in (30×20-cm) tin with oiled greaseproof paper, or baking parchment.

Cook the spinach in lightly salted boiling water for 4-5 minutes, then drain in a colander. When cool enough to handle, squeeze out all the moisture and chop roughly by hand. Turn into a bowl and add the cream, with >

Left and centre: Courgette Soufflé with Tomato and Pepper Sauce (page 33),
top: Vegetable Pâté in a Lettuce Leaf (page 34), right: Spinach Roulade.

< salt and pepper to taste. Stir in the beaten egg yolks. Whisk the egg whites to form stiff peaks and fold them in. Spread the mixture in the lined tin and dust with Parmesan. Bake for 10-12 minutes until firm in the centre.

Meanwhile, heat the tomato sauce gently to warm through, but do not let it boil.

Remove the roulade from the oven and invert the tin on to a second piece of oiled greaseproof paper or baking parchment. Lift away the tin, and peel off the lining paper. Spread the ricotta filling over the spinach base, to within ½ in (1 cm) of the edges, and roll up like a Swiss roll, using the paper to help you. Slide the roulade on to a flat serving dish. Serve cut into thick slices, accompanied by the warm tomato sauce.

GUACAMOLE

Illustrated on page 26

This is a versatile first course; delicious served with hot pitta, as part of a mixed hors d'oeuvre, or in Stuffed Tomatoes (pages 27/29).

––––––––––––– SERVES 6 –––––––––––––

3 large avocados
12 oz (340 g) tomatoes, skinned
1 large bunch spring onions
2 fresh green chillies, seeded
3 tablespoons lemon juice
1½ tablespoons olive oil
salt and freshly ground black pepper
for the garnish
5-6 crisp lettuce leaves

Chop the tomatoes, discarding the seeds and juice. Slice the spring onions finely, using the green leaves as well as the bulbs. Chop the chillies very finely.

Mix altogether in a bowl, then stir in the lemon juice and oil. Season to taste. Just before serving, peel and stone the avocados, chop finely and stir into the salad. Serve in a shallow bowl lined with lettuce leaves.

CAPONATA

Illustrated on page 29

This Mediterranean dish may be made 1-2 days in advance and kept in the refrigerator, then returned to room temperature before serving. It makes a good first course for a summer luncheon, served with homemade bread sticks. Alternatively serve with one or two other hors d'oeuvres. It goes well before baked pasta dishes.

––––––––––––– SERVES 6 –––––––––––––

1½ lb (675 g) aubergines
salt
about 6 fl oz (170 ml) olive oil
1 onion, chopped
4 stalks celery, chopped
12 oz (340 g) tomatoes, skinned and chopped
15 green olives, stoned
1½ tablespoons capers, drained
1½ tablespoons sugar
3 tablespoons white wine vinegar
freshly ground black pepper

Cut the unpeeled aubergines into ½-in (1-cm) cubes. Put them into a colander, sprinkling each layer with salt. Cover with a plate, weight down and leave for 1 hour.

Heat 3 tablespoons of the olive oil in a deep frying pan and fry the onion until it starts to colour. Add the celery and fry for a further 2 minutes, then add the tomatoes. Cook gently for about 7 minutes, then add the olives, capers, sugar, vinegar and black pepper to taste. Cook for a further 8 minutes, or until thickened. Transfer to a bowl and set aside.

Dry the aubergines in a cloth, squeezing out the moisture. Heat remaining oil in the pan, and fry the aubergines, turning often, to brown evenly. When golden brown, remove with a slotted spoon and add to the other vegetables.

Mix well, then turn into a shallow serving dish and leave to cool. Serve at room temperature, with home-made Bread Sticks (page 78), pitta or French bread.

COURGETTE SOUFFLE WITH TOMATO AND PEPPER SAUCE

Illustrated on pages 30/31

A vegetable soufflé with a contrasting sauce cannot be bettered as the start to either lunch or dinner. Roast or grilled meat would go well after this, or a baked fish; no more vegetables are required, except perhaps a few potatoes, and a green salad.

SERVES 6

1 lb (450 g) courgettes
2 oz (50 g) butter
3 tablespoons plain flour
4 fl oz (110 ml) creamy milk
2 tablespoons freshly grated Parmesan cheese
salt and freshly ground black pepper
4 large eggs, separated
for the tomato and pepper sauce
12 oz (340 g) tomatoes, skinned and chopped
1 small red pepper
1 tablespoon sunflower oil
½ oz (15 g) butter
½ bunch spring onions, sliced
a pinch of sugar (optional)

Cut the unpeeled courgettes into ½-in (1-cm) slices and cook, covered, in a little lightly salted boiling water for 10 minutes. Drain, reserving the cooking water, and push the courgettes through a coarse vegetable mill, or mash them with a fork. Return the purée to the dry pan and stir over a very low heat for a few moments, to dry out. Weigh out 6 oz (170 g) (reserve the remainder for another use).

To make the soufflé, heat the oven to 400°F (200°C, gas mark 6) and butter a 2-pint (1.2-litre) soufflé dish. Melt the butter, blend in the flour, and cook for 2 minutes. Measure out 4 fl oz (110 ml) of the courgette cooking water and heat with an equal amount of creamy milk. Add this to the roux, stir until blended, then simmer for 4 minutes. Stir in the Parmesan and salt and pepper to taste.

Add the courgette purée, stir until blended, then remove from the heat and stir in the beaten egg yolks. Set aside for 3-4 minutes, then whisk the egg whites until they form stiff peaks, and fold them into the soufflé. Turn the mixture into the soufflé dish and bake for 20 minutes, until risen and browned.

Meanwhile (or in advance if you prefer), make the sauce. Chop the skinned tomatoes. Grill the pepper until the skin is blistered and charred evenly all over. Scrape it away and chop the flesh, discarding the seeds and membrane.

Heat the oil and butter in a frying pan and cook the spring onions for 1-2 minutes, then add the chopped tomatoes and pepper. Cook all together for 5-8 minutes, depending on the ripeness of the tomatoes, seasoning with salt and pepper, and a little sugar if the tomatoes are not fully ripe. Allow to cool slightly, then process briefly in a blender or food processor to make a slightly chunky, not smooth, purée. Pour into a bowl and serve with the soufflé.

SALADE TIEDE WITH GOAT'S CHEESE

Illustrated on the cover

This pretty mixed salad, with one cooked ingredient, may be followed by almost anything, except another salad. Serve with Melba Toast (page 54).

—————————— SERVES 6 ——————————

12 small leaves batavia, or curly endive
12 leaves radicchio
1 leek, white part only
1 carrot or 1 small turnip
1 small bulb fennel
12 rosettes lamb's lettuce or small sprigs of watercress
3 oz (85 g) button mushrooms, caps only
6 × 1-in (2.5-cm) slices goat's cheese
3 plums, stoned and sliced
for the dressing
1½ tablespoons lemon juice
1½ tablespoons white wine vinegar
3 tablespoons olive oil
3 tablespoons sunflower oil
salt and freshly ground black pepper

First prepare the salad. Wash the batavia, or endive, and radicchio and shake and pat dry. Arrange on 6 plates.

Cut the leek, carrot and fennel into slices 1½-in (4-cm) thick, then cut each slice lengthways into slivers, like very thin matchsticks. Place all together in a small strainer and lower into a saucepan of boiling water. Cook for exactly 1 minute, then refresh under cold running water. Shake off excess water and set aside.

Scatter the lamb's lettuce or watercress over the other salad leaves, then slice the mushroom caps thinly and lay among the leaves and the vegetables over the top. Mix the dressing ingredients in a bowl.

Shortly before serving brush the goat's cheese with olive oil. Place the slices under a hot grill for a few moments, just until they start to melt, then transfer to the plates of salad. Spoon a little dressing over each salad. Garnish with the plums.

VEGETABLE PATE IN A LETTUCE LEAF

Illustrated on pages 30/31

Any roast or grilled meat, poultry or game would go well after these delicate vegetable quenelles.

—————————— SERVES 6 ——————————

8 oz (225 g) red lentils
12 oz (340 g) carrots
12 oz (340 g) courgettes
1½ tablespoons plain flour
salt and freshly ground black pepper
1 large egg, beaten
24 round lettuce leaves
for the sauce
1 small clove garlic, crushed
a pinch of salt
¼ pint (150 ml) fromage blanc or quark
2½ fl oz (75 ml) plain yoghurt
½ tablespoon each chopped tarragon, chervil, chives and parsley

Put the lentils into a saucepan with ¾ pint (420 ml) water. Bring to the boil and simmer, covered, for 45 minutes until very tender and mushy. Push through a medium food mill to make a coarse purée and weigh (there should be 12 oz (340 g)).

Cook the carrots and courgettes separately in boiling salted water, then drain well and grate coarsely. Mix the grated vegetables with the lentil purée, beating with a wooden spoon. Stir in the flour and season with plenty of salt and pepper. Stir in the beaten egg.

Tip the mixture into a bowl and set it in a saucepan of boiling water coming halfway up the sides of the bowl. Cover and cook for 15 minutes, then remove the bowl and leave to cool.

When the mixture is cool, lay the lettuce leaves in a steamer and steam for 30 seconds. Spread them out on a board. Using a dessertspoon, take scoops of the vegetable mixture and form into oval egg shapes, rolling them on a lightly floured board. (You should have about 24.) Wrap each one in a lettuce leaf. >

< To make the sauce, put the crushed garlic into a bowl with the salt and mash together with the back of a wooden spoon. Gradually mix in the fromage blanc, then the yoghurt, beating well to blend, and add black pepper to taste. Finally stir in the herbs and turn into a small bowl. Keep at room temperature (do not chill).

Shortly before serving, steam the filled lettuce leaves, joined sides down, for 5 minutes. (You will probably need to do them in batches, keeping the first batch warm in a serving dish while you steam the remainder.) Serve accompanied by the sauce.

CELERY REMOULADE WITH CARROT AND FENNEL SALAD

Illustrated on page 36

These salads of grated vegetables with different dressings may be followed by almost any hot dish.

--- SERVES 6 ---

for the celery remoulade
2 small heads celery
2 hard-boiled eggs, yolks only
2 raw egg yolks
salt and freshly ground black pepper
1 tablespoon Dijon mustard
2 tablespoons white wine vinegar
2 tablespoons tarragon vinegar
½ pint (280 ml) sunflower oil
¼ pint (150 ml) fromage blanc or quark
for the carrot and fennel salad
12 oz (340 g) carrots
8 oz (225 g) fennel, inner parts only
3 tablespoons sunflower oil
1½ tablespoons sesame oil
3 tablespoons lemon juice
3 tablespoons sesame seeds
12 round lettuce leaves

To make the celery remoulade, scrub the celery, discarding the tough outer stalks. Cut the tender stalks into thin strips, reserving any leaves for the garnish.

Put the hard-boiled egg yolks into a bowl and mash to a paste with the back of a wooden spoon. Beat in the raw egg yolks, mashing them in until amalgamated. Add a pinch of salt and pepper and stir in the mustard. Then gradually add the vinegar, beating all the time. Now add the oil drop by drop, as if making mayonnaise. When all the oil is absorbed, taste and adjust the seasoning: the flavour should be quite sharp. Beat in the fromage blanc, then fold in the celery strips. Set aside.

To make the carrot and fennel salad, grate the carrots and fennel fairly coarsely. Mix them in a large bowl and stir in the oils and lemon juice. Roast the sesame seeds in a dry frying pan over a low heat, stirring constantly, until light golden. Stir half of them into the salad.

To serve, arrange 2 round lettuce leaves on each of 6 individual serving plates. Pile the celery remoulade on one leaf and the carrot and fennel salad on the other. Chop the reserved celery leaves and scatter over the remoulade: scatter the reserved sesame seeds over the carrot and fennel salad. Serve with Bread Sticks (page 78), or Melba Toast (page 54).

Top: Celery Remoulade with Carrot and Fennel Salad (page 35), centre: Duck Breasts with Walnut Salad, below: Grilled Pepper and Tomato Salad.

GRILLED PEPPER
AND TOMATO SALAD

This is a beautiful dish, in glowing shades of red, yellow, and green. It can be served alone, or as part of a mixed hors d'oeuvre. Accompanied by a dish of hard-boiled eggs and sliced salami, together with some black olives, this makes a delicious summer first course.

SERVES 6

3 large yellow peppers
3 large green peppers
3 large beefsteak tomatoes, skinned
2-3 tablespoons good olive oil
½ tablespoon white wine vinegar
12 anchovy fillets
4 tablespoons milk
fresh ground black pepper
for the garnish (optional)
a few green stuffed olives, sliced

Grill the peppers, turning them frequently until they are charred and blistered evenly all over. Scrape away the skin with a small knife, rinsing off the last bits under the cold tap. Discard the stalks, seeds, and inner membranes, and cut the flesh into oval shapes, like the petals of a flower. Pat dry with kitchen paper,

Cut a small slice off the top of each tomato, scoop out and discard the inner pulp, seeds and juice, and cut the outer flesh into similar petal shapes.

Arrange the pepper and tomato petals on a flat round serving dish, radiating out from the centre. Dribble over the olive oil, sprinkle with the vinegar, and set aside for about 30 minutes.

Meanwhile, soak the anchovy fillets in milk for 20 minutes then drain them, rinse with cold water and pat dry. Arrange them over the peppers and tomatoes, garnish with the olive slices, if desired, and serve as soon as is convenient. Serve with Bread Sticks (page 78), or Onion Bread (page 77).

DUCK BREASTS
WITH WALNUT SALAD

This makes an elegant first course for a dinner party; it is quite sustaining without being heavy or over-rich. It is good followed by pasta or fish in a creamy sauce.

SERVES 6

4 duck breasts
1 tablespoon sunflower oil
for the salad
12 small leaves batavia, or curly endive
12 leaves radicchio
12 tiny sprigs watercress
1 head chicory, outer leaves removed
for the dressing
1½ tablespoons white wine vinegar
1½ tablespoons lemon juice
3 tablespoons walnut oil
3 tablespoons sunflower oil
for the garnish
2 oz (50 g) shelled walnuts, coarsely chopped

Heat the grill to moderate. Rub the duck breasts with a very little oil and grill, skin side uppermost, for 6-8 minutes. Turn and grill for a further 4-5 minutes. Set aside to cool for 30 minutes.

Meanwhile, arrange the salad leaves on 6 individual plates, slightly to one side of each. Mix all the dressing ingredients in a small jug. Just before serving, mix well again and spoon lightly and evenly over the salad leaves. Sprinkle with the walnuts.

Cut the duck breasts into diagonal slices and arrange them beside the salad. Serve while the duck is still slightly warm.

SCALLOP, ARTICHOKE AND CHICORY SALAD

This may be served individually, or on a large dish. It makes an unusual first course, served at room temperature and would go well before poultry or game.

───────────── SERVES 6 ─────────────

12 large scallops
6 tinned or frozen artichoke hearts, thawed
6 heads of chicory
3 tablespoons sunflower oil
½ pint (280 ml) hot chicken stock
juice of 1 orange
salt and freshly ground black pepper
for the dressing
2 tablespoons olive oil
2 tablespoons sunflower oil
1 tablespoon white wine vinegar
1 tablespoon lemon juice
3 tablespoons chopped dill
for the garnish (optional)
slices of lemon or lime
sprigs of dill

If using tinned hearts, drain them. Gently thaw frozen hearts. Reserve.

Wash the chicory, trim the ends and remove any discoloured outer leaves. Heat the oil in a large frying pan with a lid and add the chicory in a single layer. Cook gently, turning, for 2-3 minutes, then add the stock and orange juice. Add a little salt and some black pepper, cover and simmer gently for about 12-15 minutes, until tender when pierced with a skewer. Drain and leave to cool, reserving the juices for a soup.

Steam the scallops for 4 minutes over boiling water; remove and cool. Mix the dressing ingredients.

Cut the artichoke hearts in half or into strips about 1½ × ⅓ in (3.5 cm × 7 mm) and arrange them on 6 individual serving plates. Cut the chicory in half or into 3 pieces if large, otherwise leave them whole, and add to the plates. Cut the scallops into 2 or 3 round slices, leaving the coral tongues whole, and arrange on the plates. Spoon over a little dressing, then just before serving, spoon over the remainder. Garnish, if liked.

SEAFOOD SALAD

I enjoy making this at home whenever I can find both clams and mussels together in the shops. I like to serve it an hour or two after making it, when it has only just cooled. It goes well before meat, vegetables, pasta, or grain.

───────────── SERVES 6 ─────────────

1 lb (450 g) clams, preferably small
1 lb (450 g) mussels, preferably small
1 lb (450 g) unshelled cooked prawns
8 scallops, off the shell
1½ lb (675 g) small squid, cleaned
6 tablespoons olive oil
1 onion, finely chopped
1 large clove garlic, crushed
salt and freshly ground black pepper
3 tablespoons finely chopped parsley

Put the clams into a heavy saucepan with 2 tablespoons water and steam, covered, for 3-4 minutes, until they open. Remove with a slotted spoon and strain the juice. Cook the mussels in the same way and mix the juices.

Shell the prawns and make a small amount of stock by simmering the shells for 20 minutes in lightly salted water to cover, then strain. Put the stock into a small saucepan with the clam and mussel juice and bring to the boil. Add the scallops and poach gently for 4-6 minutes, depending on their size. Drain and cool.

Heat half the oil in a frying pan with a lid and fry the onion and garlic until they begin to colour. Cut the squid bodies into ¼-in (2.5-cm) lengths, and the tentacles >

Top: Scallop, Artichoke and Chicory Salad, centre: Seafood Salad, below: Spinach and Prawn Salad (page 41).

Above: Crab Salad with Mustard and Cress Open-Faced Sandwiches.

<into 1-in (2.5-cm) lengths. Add to the pan and fry gently, stirring from time to time, for 5 minutes. Add 2 tablespoons water, cover the pan and simmer for 5-10 minutes, until the squid are tender. Turn into a serving dish and leave to cool gently to room temperature..

If the clams and mussels are small, leave some in their shells, otherwise shell and chop them. Mix with the squid; reserve the unshelled molluscs for garnish.

Slice scallops, leaving the coral intact. Mix scallops and prawns with the other seafood, add remaining oil, salt and pepper to taste and stir carefully to mix.

Arrange the unshelled clams and mussels on top, and sprinkle with the parsley.

SPINACH AND PRAWN SALAD

Illustrated on page 39

This is a fresh and appetizing dish, best made in summer when spinach is at its most tender. It goes well before a rich dish, like chicken in a cream sauce, or blanquette de veau.

———————— SERVES 6 ————————

1-1½ lb (450-675 g) tender spinach leaves, stalks removed
2 lb (900 g) unshelled cooked prawns
6 tablespoons olive oil
3 tablespoons lemon juice
freshly ground black pepper
for the garnish
2 lemons, quartered

Remove the stalks from the spinach, wash the leaves well and shake dry. Pile them on 6 individual plates. Shell the prawns, rinse them in very cold water, then shake dry and lay them on the spinach.

Just before serving, dribble the olive oil, then the lemon juice over each plate, and sprinkle with black pepper. Garnish with lemon quarters, and serve with brown bread and butter.

CRAB SALAD

This is best made with frozen crab, thoroughly defrosted, as only the white meat is used. Especially nice on a hot day, it might be followed by a dish of grilled lamb cutlets.

———————— SERVES 6 ————————

1½ lb (675 g) white crabmeat
3 eggs, hard-boiled
1 small bunch spring onions, bulbs only, sliced
1 small green pepper, cored, seeded and finely chopped
2 tablespoons capers, drained
4 tablespoons lemon juice
a dash of Tabasco
salt and freshly ground black pepper
1 round lettuce, outer leaves removed
3 tablespoons chopped chives
for the garnish
a few thin chives, tied into a bunch
for serving
6 thin slices brown bread
2 oz (50 g) butter, softened
2 punnets mustard and cress

If using frozen crabmeat, drain it thoroughly, then flake into a bowl. Shell the eggs, separate the whites from the yolks, and chop the whites finely.

Stir the chopped egg whites into the crabmeat, with the spring onions and green pepper. Add the capers, lemon juice, Tabasco and salt and pepper to taste. Mix together lightly.

Line a shallow serving dish with the lettuce leaves and pile the crab salad mixture in the centre. Sieve the egg yolks and scatter over the top. Decorate with the chives.

Spread the bread with the butter and lay the mustard and cress thickly on the slices. Cut each sandwich into 2 halves, arrange on a serving plate and serve with the crab salad.

GRILLED AUBERGINE OMELETTE

Serve this before it has completely cooled. It would go well before plain roast chicken and green salad.

SERVES 6
---

1 large aubergine, cut into ½-in (1-cm) slices
3-4 tablespoons olive oil
8 large eggs
salt and freshly ground black pepper
½ oz (15 g) butter
for the tomato sauce
1½ lb (675 g) tomatoes
8 large spring onions, or 1 bunch small ones
2 tablespoons sunflower oil

To make the sauce, chop the tomatoes fairly roughly. Slice the spring onions, using the youngest leaves as well as the bulbs. Heat the oil in a frying pan and fry the spring onions for 2 minutes, then remove and add to the tomatoes. Process briefly in a food processor or coarse food mill, to give a slightly lumpy purée.

Heat the grill, rinse the aubergine slices and pat them dry with kitchen paper. Brush them with olive oil on both sides, and lay on an oiled piece of foil in the grill pan. Grill for 4 minutes on each side, until golden-brown. Drain on kitchen paper. Leave the grill on.

Break 4 of the eggs into a bowl, add salt and pepper, and beat. Heat an omelette pan, or 7-in (8-cm) shallow non-stick frying pan. Add half the butter, and when sizzling, pour in the eggs and make a flat omelette. When all the eggs are set except for a thin layer on the surface, slide under the grill for 30 seconds, or until the omelette is set. Slide on to a serving dish and cool.

Make another omelette in the same way with the remaining eggs, and slide on to a plate. Leave to cool for about 30 minutes.

Cut the aubergine slices into strips about ¾ in (2 cm) wide and lay them over the first omelette. Place the second omelette on top. Pour the tomato sauce around. Serve immediately, cut into wedges.

CODDLED EGGS IN GREEN SAUCE

This is an unusual hot egg dish, which looks pretty served in shallow white china bowls. Light and summery, it would go well before a roast leg of lamb.

SERVES 6
---

2 bunches watercress
1 pint (560 ml) hot chicken stock, preferably homemade
1½ oz (40 g) butter
2 tablespoons plain flour
¼ pint (150 ml) single cream
salt and freshly ground black pepper
6 large eggs
2 tablespoons freshly grated Parmesan cheese

Chop the watercress coarsely, with the stalks. Put it into a small saucepan with ¾ pint (420 ml) of the chicken stock, bring to the boil, then simmer for 5 minutes. Remove from the heat and allow to cool for a few moments, then process in a blender or food processor to make a smooth purée.

In a clean saucepan, melt 1 oz (25 g) of the butter and blend in 1 tablespoon of the flour. Cook for 1 minute, stirring, then pour in the hot watercress purée and stir until blended. Simmer for 2-3 minutes, then stir in 2 tablespoons of the cream. Season to taste with salt and pepper, and keep warm.

Boil the eggs for exactly 5 minutes, then cool and shell them. Keep them warm in a bowl of hot water.

Melt the remaining butter in a small saucepan and stir in the remaining flour. Stir for a moment, then pour in ¼ pint (150 ml) of the stock and stir until blended. Simmer gently for 3 minutes, then add the remaining cream and the Parmesan. Stir until the cheese has melted, adding salt and pepper to taste.

Place the eggs in 6 shallow bowls – or a large shallow serving dish – and pour the watercress purée over and around them. Dribble the cream sauce over the top, and serve as soon as possible.

Clockwise, from left: Grilled Aubergine Omelette served with a simple green salad, right: Coddled Eggs in Green Sauce.

EGGS WITH TAPENADE

Illustrated on page 47

In this version of a Provençal dish, the tapenade is combined with hard-boiled eggs for a piquant hors d'oeuvre.

SERVES 6
---

1 fresh French baguette
4 oz (100 g) anchovy fillets, drained
3 tablespoons milk
8 oz (225 g) black olives, stoned
8 oz (225 g) capers, drained
4 oz (100 g) tuna fish, drained
1 tablespoon mustard powder
½ pint (280 ml) olive oil
3 tablespoons brandy
¼ teaspoon each ground black pepper, ground cloves, nutmeg or mace
9 large eggs
for the garnish
a few capers
a few black olives, sliced
a sprig of fresh marjoram (optional)

Heat the oven to 275°F (140°C, gas mark 1). Cut the bread into 4-5-in (10-13-cm) lengths, split them in half, and place in the oven until crisp and golden-brown.

Soak the anchovy fillets for 10 minutes in the milk, then drain and place in a food processor or blender with the olives, capers, tuna fish and mustard. Process to make a smooth paste.

Turn the mixture into a bowl and add the oil very slowly, at first drop by drop, then in a thin trickle, stirring constantly, as if making mayonnaise. Stir in the brandy and the spices. Spread on a flat serving dish to serve.

Hard-boil the eggs, then plunge into cold water. Shell them and cut in half lengthways. Arrange cut side down, while still warm, on the tapenade. Garnish each with a few capers, olive slices, and a sprig of fresh marjoram, if available. Serve with the hot bread.

SMOKED HADDOCK SOUFFLES WITH HORSERADISH AND WATERCRESS SAUCE

Illustrated on page 47

This soufflé of smoked fish is cooked in individual dishes, and served with a contrasting sauce. Serve something plain afterwards, perhaps a cold chicken salad.

SERVES 6
---

10 oz (275 g) smoked haddock
½ pint (280 ml) milk
1½ oz (40 g) butter
2 tablespoons plain flour
2 tablespoons freshly grated Parmesan cheese
4 medium eggs, separated
freshly ground black pepper
butter, for greasing
for the sauce
¼ oz (7 g) watercress leaves
¼ pint (150 ml) fromage blanc or quark
4 tablespoons plain yoghurt
3 tablespoons double cream
4 teaspoons grated horseradish
1 teaspoon Dijon mustard

To make the sauce, chop the watercress finely in a food processor, or by hand. Add the fromage blanc, yoghurt and cream and process again or mix well in a bowl, until thoroughly blended. Add the horseradish and mustard and mix once more. Turn into a small bowl; reserve.

To make the soufflés, generously butter 6 small soufflé dishes. Heat the oven to 350°F (180°C, gas mark 4). Cut the haddock into 4 pieces and put them into a wide saucepan. Add the milk and enough cold water to barely cover. Bring to the boil, then reduce the heat, cover and cook gently for 12 minutes.

Lift out the haddock, strain the cooking liquid and measure out ⅓ pint (200 ml). Set aside. Flake the haddock, discarding skin and bone. Weigh the flesh (there should be 6 oz (170 g) and chop finely.

Melt the butter in a clean saucepan, blend in the flour and cook for 1 minute, stirring. Gradually stir in the measured fish stock and bring to the boil, stirring. Simmer for 3 minutes until thickened. Stir in the Parmesan cheese and season to taste with pepper, then stir in the chopped fish.

Remove from the heat. Beat the egg yolks lightly and stir into the mixture. Allow to cool for a few moments, then whisk the egg whites until they form stiff peaks and fold into the mixture. Fill the prepared soufflé dishes two-thirds full with the mixture.

Bake for 15 minutes, until nicely risen and just set. Serve immediately, accompanied by the sauce.

GREEN PEA MOUSSE WITH MUSHROOM SAUCE

Illustrated on page 47

These little green mousses with their mushroom sauce make a light and delicate starter. A roast leg of lamb would go well after this to make a perfect summer meal.

────────── SERVES 6 ──────────

1 lb (450 g) shelled green peas, fresh or frozen
4 tablespoons double cream
4 tablespoons fromage blanc or quark
2 large eggs, separated
salt and freshly ground black pepper
butter, for greasing
for the sauce
½ oz (15 g) dried mushrooms
8 oz (225 g) cultivated flat mushrooms
½ pint (280 ml) chicken stock
salt and freshly ground black pepper
3 tablespoons (75 ml) crème fraîche, sour cream, fromage blanc, or quark
2 tablespoons coarsely chopped flat-leaved parsley

To make the sauce, soak the dried mushrooms for 30 minutes in ¼ pint (150 ml) of the chicken stock. Drain, reserving the stock, and chop the soaked mushrooms. Wipe the fresh mushrooms, chop the caps coarsely and slice the stalks.

Put the fresh mushrooms into a saucepan with the remaining chicken stock and the stock used to soak the mushrooms. Bring to the boil, then reduce the heat and simmer for 10 minutes. Add the chopped soaked mushrooms and cook gently for a further 5 minutes. Add the crème fraîche and season to taste with salt and pepper. Simmer for another 2-3 minutes, then set aside.

To make the mousses, generously butter 6 × ¼-pint (150-ml) dariole moulds. Heat the oven to 350°F (180°C, gas mark 4). Cook the peas briefly, until just tender, in a minimum of lightly salted water. Drain, then process the peas briefly in a blender or food processor. Add the cream and fromage blanc and process again. Turn the mixture into a bowl.

Beat the egg yolks lightly and stir into the mixture. Season to taste with salt and pepper. Whisk the egg whites until they form stiff peaks and fold them into the mixture.

Pour the mixture into the greased moulds, allowing a little room for them to rise. Stand them in a roasting tin, pour in boiling water to come halfway up the sides of the moulds and bake for 35 minutes, until risen and just firm.

Shortly before the mousses are ready, reheat the sauce and stir in the parsley. Turn the moulds out on to individual plates and pour the sauce around them. Serve immediately.

EGGS IN PASTRY CASES

A delicious first course, well worth the little extra trouble it involves. The eggs may be either poached or soft-boiled. Follow this with something that can be made in advance, such as a cold fish dish, or cold roast duck, or game.

————————— SERVES 6 —————————

for the pastry
8 oz (225 g) plain flour
a pinch of salt
4 oz (120 g) chilled butter
4-5 tablespoons iced water
for the glaze
1 egg yolk
1 tablespoon milk
for the filling
6 tablespoons freshly cooked long-grain rice
6 small eggs
for the curry sauce
1 oz (25 g) butter
1 teaspoon light curry powder
½ tablespoon plain flour
1 sachet powdered saffron
6 fl oz (170 ml) hot chicken stock
salt and freshly ground black pepper
4 tablespoons double cream
for the garnish
a sprig of fresh coriander or parsley

First make the pastry. Sift the flour with the salt into a mixing bowl, add the butter cut into flakes and rub in with the fingertips until the mixture resembles fine breadcrumbs. Add the iced water and mix to a dough. (Or make the pastry in a food processor.) Wrap the dough in clingfilm and chill in the refrigerator for 20 minutes.

Heat the oven to 400°F (200°C, gas mark 6). Roll out the pastry thinly and use to line 6 small tartlet tins, about 3 in (7.5 cm) in diameter. Line with foil and weight down with dried beans, then bake blind for 6 minutes. Remove the beans, brush the pastry with the egg yolk beaten with the milk and bake for a further 8-10 minutes, or until golden-brown. Remove from the oven, set aside and turn the heat down to 300°F (150°C, gas mark 2).

To make the sauce, melt the butter in a small saucepan, blend in the curry powder and the flour, and cook for 1-2 minutes, stirring. Stir the saffron powder into the stock, then gradually add to the butter and flour mixture, stirring until blended. Add salt and pepper to taste and cook for 2-3 minutes, stirring from time to time. Stir in the cream and set aside.

Divide the rice equally among the pastry cases and reheat in the oven for 5 minutes.

Meanwhile, poach the eggs and drain on a cloth. Or cook in boiling water for exactly 5 minutes, not a second more, then plunge into cold water and peel off shells. Keep the shelled eggs hot, if necessary, in a bowl of hot water, then drain on a cloth.

To serve, place an egg on its bed of rice in each pastry case. Reheat the curry sauce and pour a little over each egg. Serve immediately, each egg garnished with a sprig of coriander or parsley.

Above: Green Pea Mousse with Mushroom Sauce (page 45).

Above: Eggs in Pastry Cases.

Above: Eggs with Tapenade (page 44).

Above: Smoked Haddock Soufflé (page 44).

SOLE GOUJONS WITH FRIED PARSLEY

This is a classic dish, traditionally served with a sauce tartare. This more unusual version partners it with a fresh tomato sauce.

―――――― SERVES 6 ――――――

12 Dover or lemon sole fillets weighing about 2½ lb (1.1 kg), skinned
2 eggs, beaten
1 tablespoon milk
dry white breadcrumbs
vegetable oil for frying
12 large sprigs of parsley
3 lemons, cut into quarters
for the sauce
fresh tomato sauce (see Cannelloni page 15)
1 tablespoon sunflower oil
1 teaspoon finely chopped fresh ginger root
2 tablespoons fresh orange juice
2 tablespoons lemon juice

Make the sauce in advance, using the tomato sauce on page 15 as a base. To this add another tablespoon of fresh oil, the ginger, orange and lemon juice. Process once more, to a coarse purée, and pour into a serving bowl. Cover and chill in the refrigerator for 1-2 hours.

Wash the sole fillets and pat dry in a cloth. Cut them diagonally into strips about ½ in (1 cm) wide. Beat the eggs with the milk and pour into a shallow dish. Dip each sole goujon first in the egg mixture, then coat with breadcrumbs. Lay them side by side on a large plate.

Heat the oil in a deep-fryer or wok to 360°F (185°C). Add the goujons in small batches, and fry for about 3 minutes, turning once, until golden brown. Remove, drain on kitchen paper and transfer to a heated serving dish. Reheat the oil before frying the next batch.

When all the goujons are fried, fry the parsley for 30 seconds, just until crisp. Drain and then use as garnish with the lemon quarters. Serve with the sauce.

FILETS DE SOLE DUGLERE

This is a speciality of the Savoy Hotel, an elegant dish that can be served either hot or cold. It is best followed by something very simple: a chicken salad, cold roast duck with a salad of mixed leaves, or grilled lamb cutlets.

―――――― SERVES 6 ――――――

4 Dover or lemon soles weighing about 1 lb (450 g) each, skinned and each filleted into 4, with their bones
1 small onion, halved
1 small carrot, halved
1 stalk celery, halved
3 stalks parsley
1 small bay leaf
salt
6 black peppercorns
1 oz (25 g) butter
3 shallots, finely chopped
4 tomatoes, skinned, seeded and finely chopped
1 tablespoon finely chopped parsley
white pepper
4 fl oz (110 ml) dry white wine
1 teaspoon plain flour
4 tablespoons double cream

Make a fish stock by putting the fish bones into a saucepan with the onion, carrot, celery, parsley, bay leaf, salt, peppercorns and add water just to cover. Bring to the boil, then reduce the heat and simmer for 20 minutes. Strain and measure out 4 fl oz (110 ml); reserve the remaining stock for another dish.

Divide each sole fillet in half diagonally. Heat the butter in a large heavy frying pan with a lid and fry the shallots gently until they begin to colour, then add the tomatoes and parsley. Cook for 1 minute, season with salt and pepper, then remove from the heat.

Lay the sole fillets on top of the tomatoes, and pour over the measured fish stock and wine. Cover and simmer for 5-6 minutes, until just cooked, then just >

Top: Goujons of Sole with Fried Parsley, below: Filets de Sole Dugléré.

< transfer the fish to a shallow serving dish. If serving hot, cover and keep warm.

Stir the flour into the cream in a small bowl, beating until smooth, then add to the pan and cook over a low heat, stirring constantly, for 3-4 minutes, then pour over the fish fillets if serving hot, and serve immediately.

If serving cold, pour the sauce into a bowl and stand it in a sink half full of cold water, stirring often to prevent a skin from forming, leave until it has reached room temperature, then pour over the fish. The dish may be kept in the refrigerator for a few hours, but should be served at room temperature.

FISH QUENELLES IN SPINACH LEAVES

These little bundles, wrapped in green leaves and steamed, accompanied by hollandaise sauce, make a very appealing first course. They could also be served with the Tomato and Pepper Sauce on page 33. A joint of roast meat, perhaps a leg of lamb, or a rolled sirloin of beef, would go very nicely after this.

———— SERVES 5-6 ————

1½ lb (675 g) haddock fillets
2 large egg whites, lightly beaten
4 oz (120 g) fromage blanc or quark
¼ pint (150 ml) double cream
salt and freshly ground black pepper
about 24 spinach leaves
a little flour for dusting
for the hollandaise sauce
6 egg yolks
a pinch of salt
8 oz (225 g) unsalted butter, diced
1 tablespoon lemon juice

Skin the haddock fillets and chop into pieces. Place in a food processor and process until reduced to small pieces. Add the egg whites and process until >

Left: Fish Quenelles in Spinach Leaves,
right: Escabeche (page 52).

<smooth. Then add the fromage blanc and cream, and process again until thoroughly blended. Season to taste with salt and pepper. Turn into a bowl, cover with clingfilm and chill for 1-2 hours.

Meanwhile, blanch the spinach leaves in boiling water for 1 minute, then drain thoroughly and spread out on a board.

When the fish mixture is chilled, use a large teaspoon to scoop out egg-shaped quenelles, shaping them lightly on a lightly floured board, and wrap each one in a spinach leaf. (They should weigh about 1 oz (25 g) each, and you should have about 24.)

Shortly before serving, bring a wide saucepan of water, or a wok, to the boil. Lay half the spinach bundles in a steamer and place over the boiling water. Cook for 4 minutes, then transfer to a heated serving dish and keep warm while you steam the remainder.

While the quenelles are cooking, make the sauce. Heat the container of the food processor by filling it with very hot water and leaving to stand for 5 minutes, then empty it and dry well. Put in the egg yolks with the salt and process for 30 seconds.

Melt the butter in a small saucepan and heat until almost boiling, then add the lemon juice. Pour slowly through the lid on to the egg yolks, with the machine running, until all the butter is absorbed and the sauce is thickened. (If by any chance the sauce fails to thicken, pour it into a bowl standing over a pan of simmering water and stir constantly until thickened.) Tip the sauce into a warm bowl and serve with the quenelles.

ESCABECHE

Illustrated on page 50/51

This dish of pickled fish is an extremely useful one, for it must be made 2-3 days in advance, with no further preparation before serving. It makes a good start to a summer meal, and can be followed by any dish of poultry or meat, pasta, rice, or vegetables.

--- **SERVES 6** ---

2 lb (900 g) halibut steaks, about ¾ in (2 cm) thick, or other firm white fish
6 fl oz (170 ml) olive oil
2 large onions, thinly sliced
2 large carrots, coarsely grated
1 dried chilli, finely chopped
2 large cloves garlic, finely chopped
2 bay leaves, crumbled
1 teaspoon sea salt
8 black peppercorns, roughly crushed
6 fl oz (170 ml) white wine vinegar
3 tablespoons chopped parsley

Start 2-3 days in advance. Heat half the oil in a large heavy frying pan and fry the fish gently for 4-5 minutes on each side, then drain on kitchen paper and leave to cool.

Pour away the oil and clean the pan. Divide the onion slices into rings, and fry them gently in the remaining oil for about 5 minutes, until soft, but not coloured, then add the carrots, chilli, garlic, bay leaves, salt, peppercorns and vinegar. Cook all together for 5 minutes, then spoon half the mixture into a broad, shallow dish.

Divide the fish into 6 pieces, discarding skin and bone, and lay on the vegetable mixture. Cover with the remaining mixture and leave to cool.

Cover the dish with clingfilm and chill in the bottom of the refrigerator for 2-3 days. Remove 1-2 hours before serving, and leave to come to room temperature. Sprinkle with the parsley and serve accompanied by wholemeal rolls and butter.

SALMON MOULDS WITH DILL SAUCE

Illustrated on page 55

This dish is an adaptation of a recipe by the late James Beard, one of the most distinguished of American food writers. It is usually made as a loaf, but I like to make small moulds, one for each person, and serve them with a dill sauce. The Saffron Sauce on page 70, with 3 tablespoons chopped chives added, is also delicious as an accompaniment. This is a substantial first course, and is lengthy to prepare, so choose something light to follow; a salad is really all that is required, perhaps with some prosciutto.

SERVES 6

1½ lb (675 g) salmon
½ onion, stuck with 2 cloves
1 carrot, cut in quarters
1 stalk celery, cut in half
1 bay leaf
salt
6 black peppercorns
¼ pint (150 ml) dry white wine or 4 tablespoons dry white vermouth
7 oz (200 g) long-grain rice
sea salt and freshly ground black pepper
2 large eggs, lightly beaten
6 tablespoons milk
butter for greasing
for the dill sauce
1½ oz (40 g) butter
2 tablespoons plain flour
½ pint (280 ml) fish stock (see method)
4 fl oz (110 ml) crème fraîche, fromage blanc or quark
½ teaspoon Dijon mustard
3 tablespoons finely chopped dill
for the garnish
sprigs of dill

Put the piece of salmon into a saucepan that fits it as closely as possible. Pour in cold water to just cover and add the onion, carrot, celery, bay leaf, salt, black pepper-corns and wine. Bring to the boil, then reduce the heat, and simmer, covered, for about 5 minutes. Turn off the heat and leave the salmon to cool in its stock.

Later, or the next day, remove the salmon, leaving the rest of the ingredients in the pan. Take the fish off the bone, remove the skin and set aside. Return the skin and bones to the pan and bring back to the boil. Cook for 30 minutes, then strain and leave to cool.

Cook the rice in boiling salted water until only just cooked, then drain well, and tip into a large bowl. Flake the salmon and mix with the rice. Season to taste with salt and pepper. Stir in the eggs and milk.

Heat the oven to 350°F (180°C, gas mark 4).

Grease 6 × ¼-pint (150-ml) ovenproof moulds with butter. Spoon the salmon mixture into the moulds, smoothing the tops evenly, and cover with pieces of foil. Stand in a roasting tin, pour in boiling water to come halfway up the sides of the moulds and bake for 30 minutes until firm.

Meanwhile, make the sauce. Melt the butter in a saucepan, blend in the flour, and cook, stirring, for 1 minute. Reheat ½ pint (280 ml) of the strained fish stock and gradually add to the roux, stirring until blended and smooth. Simmer for 1-2 minutes. If using crème fraîche, stir the mustard into it and add to the pan. Return to the boil, then simmer gently for a further 2 minutes. If using fromage blanc or quark, remove the pan from the heat and stir in; do not boil again or the sauce will separate.

Season the sauce with salt and pepper to taste, then stir in the chopped dill. Cover and keep warm.

To serve, run a knife round the edge of the salmon moulds and unmould on to individual plates, giving the base of each mould a sharp tap as you do so. Do not worry if the moulds come apart; they can be easily remoulded into shape. Spoon a little of the sauce around each one, and serve the rest separately, in a small jug or sauceboat. Garnish with sprigs of dill.

FISH TERRINE WITH PUREE OF GREEN PEAS

A hot fish terrine makes a perfect start for a formal dinner. It could be followed to advantage by a simple meat dish, possibly a roast rack of lamb.

———————— SERVES 6 ————————

1 lb (450 g) haddock fillets, skinned (skinned weight)
2 egg whites, lightly beaten
4 oz (120 g) fromage blanc or quark
¼ pint (150 ml) double cream
1 teaspoon sea salt
freshly ground black pepper
butter for greasing
for the pea purée
8 oz (225 g) shelled peas, fresh or frozen
2 tablespoons double cream
2 eggs, lightly beaten
salt and freshly ground black pepper
for the fresh tomato sauce
1 lb (450 g) tomatoes, skinned and quartered
½ bunch spring onions, bulbs only, sliced
1 tablespoon sunflower oil

Chop the haddock and place in a food processor. Process until reduced to small pieces, then add the egg whites and process until blended. Add the fromage blanc, cream, salt and pepper, and process until smooth. Turn the mixture into a bowl, cover with clingfilm and chill for 1-2 hours.

Meanwhile, cook the peas briefly in boiling salted water until just tender. Drain and place in the food processor. Add the cream and process until blended. Add the beaten eggs and process again. Season to taste with salt and pepper. Pour into an ovenproof bowl and cover with foil.

Heat the oven to 350°F (180°C, gas mark 4).

Butter a loaf tin of about 1¼ pint (750 ml) capacity. Turn the fish mixture into the tin and cover with foil.

Stand the tin and the bowl with the pea purée in a roasting tin. Pour in boiling water to come halfway up the sides of the tin and bowl. Bake for 45 minutes, or until the fish terrine is firm when pressed lightly in the centre.

To make the sauce, place the tomatoes in the food processor and reduce to a chunky purée. Soften the spring onions in the oil for 2 minutes, then add to the tomatoes and process again, until reduced to a coarse purée. Turn into a small saucepan and just warm through.

When the fish terrine is cooked, run a knife round the edge and unmould it on to a flat serving dish. Using a palette knife, spread the pea purée over the top or, if preferred, spoon it on the serving dish and arrange the terrine on top. Serve the terrine cut into thick slices, accompanied by the sauce in a sauceboat.

MELBA TOAST

This delicate accompaniment to soups, salads, and dishes of all sorts always reminds me of the Hotel Ritz in Paris, which must have been the first place I ever had it. I have never been able to make it as well as they did, but am grateful to Prue Leith for allowing me to copy her method, which is the best I've found.

Heat the oven to 250°F (120°C, gas mark ½).

Cut dry white or brown bread into very thin slices and toast them lightly on both sides. Then cut off the crusts and carefully split each slice of toast through, so that you have two even-thinner slices. Lay the slices, toasted-side down, on a baking sheet and bake for 1 hour. Serve after cooling, but the same day as made.

Top: Fish Terrine with Purée of Green Peas, below: Salmon Moulds with Dill Sauce (page 53) and Melba Toast.

Left: Small Fish Kebabs, right: Gravlax with Mustard and Dill Sauce.

GRAVLAX WITH MUSTARD AND DILL SAUCE

This Scandinavian delicacy of cured raw salmon is becoming almost as popular as smoked salmon in this country. It is not hard to make at home, so long as you can obtain dill, which is used in fairly generous amounts. Once made, gravlax can be kept for up to a week in the refrigerator, or frozen. Almost anything goes well after it: meat, poultry, game, or another fish.

―――――― SERVES 6-8 ――――――

3¼ lb (1.5 kg) middle cut of salmon
6 oz (225 g) fresh dill, stalks and leaves, coarsely chopped
2 tablespoons white peppercorns, coarsely crushed
2 oz (50 g) sea salt
2 oz (50 g) granulated sugar
for the mustard and dill sauce
3 tablespoons Dijon mustard
2 tablespoons caster sugar
2 tablespoons white wine vinegar
6-8 tablespoons olive oil
3 tablespoons finely chopped dill

Ask the fishmonger to cut the piece of salmon in half horizontally, and to remove the backbone. Pull out all the small bones with tweezers. Make some small incisions in the skin with a small sharp knife. Lay 2 oz (50 g) of the dill in a shallow dish large enough to hold the salmon. Put one salmon half on this, skin-side down.

Pound the peppercorns with the salt and sugar in a mortar with a pestle, for 1-2 minutes. Spread half the mixture over the cut side of the salmon in the dish, then lay 2 oz (50 g) dill over it.

Spread the remaining pepper mixture over the cut side of the second piece of salmon, then lay it over the first half, skin-side uppermost, so that the salmon is reassembled. Spread 2 oz (50 g) dill over the top and cover with a piece of foil. Lay a board on top and weight down with 3 weights of about 1 lb (450 g) each. Chill in the refrigerator for 2-3 days, turning the pieces of fish each day.

To make the sauce, put the mustard into a small bowl and stir in the sugar and vinegar to make a thin paste. Then start adding the oil, very gradually drop by drop, as if making a mayonnaise. When half the oil is absorbed, add the remainder in a thin trickle. Stir in the chopped dill, spoon into a small dish and serve separately.

SMALL FISH KEBABS

I have a set of short skewers specially for making this dish, as I like to serve 2, or even 3, per person. It also makes a lovely dish, either on its own or combined with one or two other fish hors d'oeuvres for a special occasion, such as Steamed Scallops (page 58), and Stuffed Mussels (page 58).

―――――― SERVES 6 ――――――

2¼ lb (1 kg) firm white fish such as conger eel, monkfish or halibut, filleted and skinned
4 tablespoons olive oil
2 tablespoons lemon juice
2 shallots, finely chopped
2 tablespoons chopped parsley
freshly ground black pepper
for the garnish
thin lime slices

Cut the fish into neat 1-in (2.5-cm) squares. Put them into a bowl and add the oil and lemon juice. Gently stir in the shallot and parsley, season with pepper and leave to marinate for 3-4 hours, stirring occasionally.

Just before serving, heat the grill to moderate and thread the pieces of fish on to small greased skewers, about 4 pieces to each skewer. Grill carefully for about 12 minutes, turning often and basting with the remaining marinade. Transfer to a serving dish, fold over the thin lime slices and thread through the pith onto the end of the skewer. Serve immediately.

STUFFED MUSSELS

This is a delicious first course, quite fiddly to make, but well worth the effort. It also can be made in half quantities and served with one or two other dishes, like Small Fish Kebabs (page 57) and Steamed Scallops. Any dish of meat, poultry, or game would go well after this, either plainly roasted or grilled, or in a sauce.

─────────── SERVES 6 ───────────

6 lb (2.8 kg) mussels
¼ pint (150 ml) dry white wine
4 oz (120 g) butter
4 shallots, finely chopped
2 cloves garlic, finely chopped
4 oz (120 g) dry white breadcrumbs
½ oz (15 g) chopped parsley
salt and freshly ground black pepper

Clean the mussels with a stiff brush, in several changes of water. Put the wine into a large saucepan with ¼ pint (150 ml) water and bring to the boil. Drop in the mussels and simmer for 4 minutes, or until they have opened. Strain off and reserve the liquid and allow the mussels to cool slightly. Then remove and discard one shell from each mussel. Keep the half shells with the meat warm.

Melt the butter in a frying pan and sauté the shallots for 1-2 minutes, then add the garlic and sauté until the shallots start to colour. Add the breadcrumbs and stir until they are light golden. Remove from the heat and stir in the parsley. Moisten with about 4 tablespoons of the strained mussel liquid and season to taste with salt and pepper. Using a large teaspoon, spoon some of the stuffing over each mussel in its shell, doming it slightly. Place them in a shallow ovenproof dish (they can be prepared in advance up to this stage).

Just before serving, heat the grill to high. Place the mussels under it, and grill until nicely browned. You will probably have to do them in batches, transferring the first batch to a heated serving platter and keeping warm while you grill the remainder. Serve as soon as possible.

STEAMED SCALLOPS

This appetizing starter might be followed by a dish in a creamy sauce, or a chicken pie.

─────────── SERVES 6 ───────────

18 large scallops
a few drops of sesame oil
1 oz (25 g) fresh root ginger, thinly sliced
2 large cloves garlic, peeled and sliced
6 large spring onions, trimmed and cut into 1½-in (3.5-cm) lengths
½ tablespoon light soy sauce
for the sauce
1½ tablespoons dry white vermouth
½ tablespoon sunflower oil
½ tablespoon sesame oil
1 tablespoon light soy sauce

Cut out 6×6-in (15-cm) squares of foil and lay them on a board. Rub each with a little sesame oil. Lay half the sliced ginger and garlic in the centre of each piece of foil. Cut the spring onion into thin slivers and divide a quarter of them between the pieces of foil.

Separate the coral from the scallops. Cut the white flesh into quarters and lay them, with their coral, on the bed of ginger, garlic, and spring onion, dividing them equally among the pieces of foil. Sprinkle with the soy sauce, cover with the remaining ginger and garlic and one-third of the remaining spring onion. Seal the edges of the foil tightly, to make parcels.

Just before serving, bring some water to the boil in a steamer. Lay the packages in the steamer, cover and cook for 8 minutes.

Meanwhile, make the sauce. Mix the vermouth, oils and soy sauce together in a small bowl.

Remove the packages from the steamer. Puncture the foil and drain the juices into the sauce, mixing well. Unwrap the foil and lay the scallops in the shells, discarding the ginger, garlic and spring onion. Give the sauce a final whisk and pour over the scallops. Sprinkle the reserved spring onion over the top and serve.

Top: Stuffed Mussels, below: Steamed Scallops.

BARBECUED SPARE RIBS WITH MUSTARD SAUCE

This makes an entertaining first course for an informal evening. Since the ribs are eaten in the fingers, large napkins are essential. Serve a light pasta dish to follow, or a fish salad.

———————— SERVES 6 ————————

3 lb (1.4 kg) spare ribs, cut up
for the marinade
1 small onion, chopped
3 tablespoons olive oil
3 tablespoons tomato purée
4 tablespoons red wine vinegar
⅓ pint (200 ml) hot chicken stock
2 tablespoons clear honey
1 teaspoon Dijon mustard
1 large clove garlic, crushed
1 teaspoon dried thyme
salt and freshly ground black pepper
a dash of Tabasco
for the mustard sauce
¼ pint (150 ml) plain yoghurt
¼ pint (150 ml) mayonnaise
2 teaspoons Dijon mustard
2 teaspoons grated horseradish
1 teaspoon lemon juice
2 teaspoons tomato purée
several dashes of Tabasco

The day before, make the marinade. Fry the onion gently in the oil until softened. Mix the tomato purée and vinegar in a cup and add to the onion, then add the stock, honey, mustard, garlic, and thyme. Season to taste with salt and pepper and bring to the boil. Cover the pan and simmer for 15 minutes, stirring often, adding a little extra stock if it gets too thick. Season with Tabasco and leave to cool.

Two hours before cooking, brush the mixture over the ribs and leave to marinate.

Meanwhile, make the mustard sauce. Beat the yoghurt until smooth, and mix with the mayonnaise. Stir in the mustard, horseradish, lemon juice, tomato purée and Tabasco to taste.

One hour before serving, line the bottom of the oven with foil, to catch any splashes. Heat it to 450°F (230°C, gas mark 8).

Line 2 roasting tins with foil and lay the ribs in them. Bake for 45 minutes (switch the tins round halfway through), turning the ribs from time to time and basting with the marinade.

To serve, pile the ribs on a large heated flat dish and place in the centre of the table, accompanied by the sauce in a separate bowl.

Left: Onion Bread (page 77), right: Barbecued Spare Ribs with Mustard Sauce.

Left: Marinated Beef with Mushrooms, right: Skewers of Chicken Breasts.

MARINATED BEEF WITH MUSHROOMS

This is an adaptation of a beautiful dish called Carpaccio, a speciality of Piedmont that I have eaten in Turin. It is appetizing and sustaining without being rich, and goes well before a dish of fish in a creamy sauce. It can also be followed by a pasta dish, or vegetables, or rice.

SERVES 6

1 lb (450 g) beef fillet, thinly sliced
8 oz (225 g) small mushrooms
6 tablespoons good olive oil
5 tablespoons lemon juice
freshly ground black pepper
1 oz (25 g) fresh Parmesan cheese
½ tablespoon very finely chopped parsley
for the garnish (optional)
2-3 lemons, cut into quarters

If you have a friendly butcher, ask him to slice the beef for you. It needs to be cut into ¼-in (6-mm) slices. If you are slicing the meat yourself, chill the fillet for several hours before slicing it; this makes it easier to cut. Lay the slices well apart between 2 pieces of clingfilm. Using a meat bat or wooden rolling pin, beat the slices out until paper-thin. Wrap in the clingfilm, and chill for several hours, until 1 hour before required.

Shortly before serving, wipe the mushrooms, remove the stalks, and slice the caps thinly. Place in a bowl. Arrange the slices of beef on a large serving plate, or on individual plates, allowing 2-3 slices to each.

Combine the oil, lemon juice and pepper and spoon a very little of it over the beef, spreading it with the fingers, just to moisten. Pour the remaining oil and lemon over the mushrooms and toss to mix.

Arrange the sliced mushrooms in a mound in the centre of the beef. Using a small, sharp knife, cut the Parmesan into very thin slivers and scatter over the mushrooms. Sprinkle a little parsley over the top. Serve soon after preparing, garnished with lemon wedges, if liked, before the dish can discolour and lose its appeal.

SKEWERS OF CHICKEN BREASTS

A small skewer of crisply cooked chicken breast, served straight from the grill, makes an admirable first course. It can be followed by almost anything except, perhaps, more meat: a fish dish, pasta, a vegetable dish, or pastry.

SERVES 6

2 lb (1 kg) boneless chicken breasts
for the marinade
3 tablespoons sunflower oil
3 tablespoons dry white vermouth
3 tablespoons light soy sauce
1 large clove garlic, finely chopped
1 in (2.5 cm) cube fresh ginger root, finely chopped
for the garnish
12 sprigs of watercress
2 lemons, cut into quarters

Several hours in advance, or the day before, cut the chicken into neat 1 in (2.5 cm) cubes and put them into a bowl. Add the oil, vermouth and soy sauce and stir well to mix, then stir in the garlic and ginger. Cover with clingfilm and chill in the refrigerator for at least 8 hours, or overnight.

Shortly before serving, heat the grill to moderate.

Thread the pieces of chicken on to 6 skewers, or 12 tiny ones. Grill for 10 minutes, turning frequently and basting with the remaining marinade. Serve as soon as possible after cooking, on a flat dish garnished with sprigs of watercress and lemon wedges.

DUCK PATE WITH PLUM SAUCE

A home-made pâté, served with a sharp fruit sauce and accompanied by warm Onion Bread (page 71) makes a welcoming start for a meal on a winter's day. Both pâté and sauce can be made in advance, leaving only the bread to be baked on the day itself. A light dish is all that is required afterwards, perhaps some grilled trout with a green salad.

─────────── SERVES 8-10 ───────────

1 duck
12 oz (340 g) unsmoked streaky bacon in 1 piece, cubed
12 oz (340 g) pork belly, cubed
12 oz (340 g) pie veal, cubed
1½ tablespoons green peppercorns
2 cloves garlic, crushed
1 tablespoon sea salt
½ teaspoon ground mace or nutmeg
7 fl oz (200 ml) dry white wine
3 tablespoons brandy
for the garnish
3 small bay leaves
a few cranberries or juniper berries
for the plum sauce
1 lb (450 g) plums, fresh or tinned
¼ pint (150 ml) port or red wine
finely grated rind of 1 orange
finely grated rind of ½ lemon
3 tablespoons redcurrant jelly
1 tablespoon Dijon mustard
2 tablespoons fresh orange juice
2 tablespoons lemon juice

Make the pâté 1-2 days before required.

Heat the oven to 400°F (200°C, gas mark 6).

Lay the duck breast-side down on a rack in a roasting tin and cook for 25 minutes, then remove from the oven and leave to cool.

Place the pork, veal and bacon in a food processor and chop finely, or put through a mincer. Mix all the >

< meats together in a large bowl.

Cut the flesh off the partly roasted duck, reserving the skin and bones for making Bortsch (page 12), or Game and Lentil Soup (page 10). Cut the meat into neat dice and stir into the other meats. Add the peppercorns, garlic, salt and mace and mix well. Stir in the wine and brandy and mix again. Cover and set aside for 1-2 hours, to allow the flavours to develop.

Heat the oven to 300°F (150°C, gas mark 2).

Arrange the bay leaves and berries decoratively in the bottom of a 2-lb (900-g) terrine mould or loaf tin. Pile in the duck mixture and smooth it with a palette knife. Stand in a roasting tin, pour in boiling water to come halfway up the sides of the terrine and cook, uncovered, for 1¾ hours.

Remove from the oven and leave to cool, then cover loosely with a piece of foil, and weight down with 2 weights of about 1½ lb (675 g) each. Leave overnight in a cool place; next day, remove the weights and chill in the refrigerator for a minimum of 8 hours. (The pâté can be kept for up to 1 week before eating.)

To make the sauce, stone the plums and chop roughly. (Tinned plums should be drained of their syrup or juice.) Put the plums into a heavy saucepan with the port, orange and lemon rind. Cook gently, uncovered, for 10 minutes, until thick and slightly jammy.

Meanwhile, melt the redcurrant jelly in a small bowl set over a pan of simmering water. Stir in the mustard, and orange and lemon juices, then remove from the heat.

Remove the plums from the heat and pour the jelly mixture on to them through a small sieve. Allow to cool to room temperature.

Unmould the pâté on to a flat dish. Serve accompanied by the plum sauce in a bowl, and warm Onion Bread.

Left: Bread Sticks (page 78), right: Duck Pâté with Plum Sauce.

GRILLED CHICKEN WINGS WITH GARLIC SAUCE

These tasty joints make an excellent first course, eaten in the fingers. They are also good, without the sauce, served with one or two other hors d'oeuvres, such as Grilled Pepper and Tomato Salad (page 37), Carrot and Fennel Salad (page 35). Make in half quantities and add 1 crushed clove garlic to the marinade.

―――――――― SERVES 6 ――――――――

3 lb (1.4 kg) chicken wings, joints only
6 tablespoons olive oil
juice of 1½ lemons
salt and freshly ground black pepper
for the garlic sauce
½ pint (280 ml) plain yoghurt
2 cloves garlic, crushed
½ teaspoon sea salt
4 tablespoons mixed chopped herbs: chives, chervil, parsley, dill
for the garnish (optional)
lemon slices
sprigs of flat-leaved parsley

Two hours before cooking, line the grill pan with foil and rub with oil. Cut each chicken wing into 2 joints, and lay in the grill pan. Pour over the oil and lemon juice, and sprinkle with salt and pepper. Leave to marinate for 2 hours, turning the joints over once or twice.

Meanwhile, make the sauce. Beat the yoghurt until smooth, then stir in the garlic and salt. Stir in all but 2 teaspoons of the herbs. Spoon the sauce into a small serving bowl and scatter the remaining herbs on top.

Shortly before serving, heat the grill to moderate.

Grill the chicken wings slowly for 8-10 minutes on each side, until well browned and just cooked through. Baste with the marinade once or twice while cooking.

Serve piled on a serving platter, garnished with lemon slices and parsley if wished, and accompanied by the garlic sauce.

CHICKEN WITH PINE NUTS

This is a pretty dish, light but sustaining, elegant enough for a dinner party. It is very quick to cook, but should not be kept waiting. It may be followed by a cold fish dish, or pasta with a vegetable sauce.

―――――――― SERVES 6 ――――――――

2 chicken breasts
2 chicken thighs
2 tablespoons olive oil
1½ teaspoons dry white vermouth
1 tablespoon light soy sauce
1 large clove garlic, crushed
6 oz (170 g) young spinach leaves
6 oz (170 g) mushrooms, caps only
2 tablespoons sesame seeds
2 tablespoons pine nuts
salt and freshly ground black pepper
1½ tablespoons finely chopped parsley

Cut the chicken flesh off the bones, discarding the skin and membranes, and cut into neat cubes. Put into a bowl and add the oil, vermouth, and half the soy sauce. Add the garlic and stir to mix. Leave to marinate for at least 1 hour, or as long as is convenient, stirring from time to time.

Shortly before serving, blanch the spinach leaves for 1 minute in boiling water, then drain in a colander. Use to line 6 small plates, and keep warm.

Chop the mushrooms neatly. Toast the sesame seeds in a dry frying pan, tossing now and then until they turn golden and start to jump about. Set aside.

Just before serving, heat a non-stick frying pan or wok and turn the chicken with its juices into it. Stir-fry for 1 minute, then add the mushrooms and stir-fry for a further 2-3 minutes, until the chicken is just cooked.

Remove from the heat and add the sesame seeds, pine nuts, the remaining soy sauce and salt and pepper to taste. Return to the heat for a moment, then divide between the 6 plates, sprinkle with parsley and serve.

Top: Grilled Chicken Wings With Garlic Sauce, below: Chicken with Pine Nuts.

Left: Spinach and Cheese Pie, right: Shellfish en Croûte.

SPINACH AND CHEESE PIE

Filo pastry is very versatile and learning to handle it is well worthwhile. Choose something simple to follow, perhaps grilled lamb cutlets with a potato purée and a green salad.

SERVES 6
---

2 lb (900 g) spinach
2 bunches large spring onions, bulbs only
1½ oz (40 g) parsley, stalks removed
4 tablespoons fresh dill
1 tablespoon sea salt
5 oz (140 g) butter
1 large onion, finely chopped
2 large eggs, beaten
4 oz (100 g) feta cheese
freshly ground black pepper
1 lb (450 g) filo pastry

Chop the spinach, spring onions, parsley and dill quite finely, either by hand or in a food processor. Layer the mixture in a large bowl, sprinkling each layer with the salt. Leave for 15-20 minutes, then squeeze to extract all the moisture and place in a clean dry bowl.

Meanwhile, melt 3 oz (85 g) of the butter in a frying pan and fry the onion gently, until pale golden. Then stir the onion into the spinach mixture and mix well. Mix in the eggs and feta with plenty of pepper but no salt.

Heat the oven to 350°F (180°C, gas mark 4).

Melt the remaining butter and use some of it to brush a 10-in (25-cm) tin about 1½ in (3.5 cm) deep. Line with a sheet of filo, trimming so that it overlaps the edges of the tin by about 1½ in (3.5 cm). Brush the filo with melted butter, then lay another sheet over it and brush with melted butter. Continue until you have 5 sheets, then cover the remaining filo with a damp cloth. Brush the top sheet of filo in the tin with melted butter, then fill the tin with the spinach mixture, spreading it out evenly. Cover with another sheet of filo, trimming this time to fit the tin exactly. Brush with more melted butter and repeat with 4 more filo sheets. When finished, fold the overlapping edges of the bottom layer of filo sheets back over the top of the pie, brushing them with melted butter so that they adhere. Brush the top with melted butter and mark in a trellis pattern with a sharp knife.

Bake for 40 minutes until golden and puffy. Serve warm, about 30 minutes after baking.

SHELLFISH EN CROUTE

Prawns cooked briefly in oil with spring onions, ginger and orange juice make a delicious filling for a crisp bread case. Follow with an egg dish, or a salad.

SERVES 6
---

2 small white loaves, 1-2 days old
2½ oz (75 g) butter, melted
for the prawn filling
6 tablespoons sunflower oil
1 large bunch spring onions, sliced, with the best of their leaves
2 tablespoons finely chopped fresh root ginger
1½ lb (675 g) peeled prawns
salt and freshly ground black pepper
juice of 2 oranges
juice of 1 lemon
3 tablespoons chopped chives

Make the croûtes exactly as for Mushrooms en Croûte (page 74), brushing them with plain melted butter. Bake as directed, and keep warm.

While the croûtes are baking, heat the oil in a large frying pan or wok and stir-fry the spring onions for 2 minutes. Add the ginger and stir-fry for 1 minute, then add the prawns and cook for 3 minutes. Add the orange and lemon juices and stir-fry for 1 further minute. Remove from the heat, and stir in half the chopped chives.

Lay the croûtes on individual plates and spoon the prawns and their juices in and around them. Sprinkle with the remaining chives.

CRAB PASTIES WITH SAFFRON SAUCE

Follow these rich pasties with a simple dish; my choice would be either a poached fish with new potatoes and a green salad, or some really good smoked ham with a lettuce and a tomato salad.

――――――― MAKES 12 ―――――――

for the pastry
9 oz (250 g) plain flour
a pinch of salt
4½ oz (130 g) butter, chilled and diced
1 teaspoon lemon juice
for the glaze
1 egg yolk
1 tablespoon milk
for the crab filling
8 oz (225 g) white crabmeat, flaked, thoroughly thawed if frozen
¼ pint (150 ml) milk
1 slice onion
¼ bay leaf
1 clove
salt and freshly ground black pepper
grated nutmeg
½ oz (15 g) butter
2 teaspoons plain flour
2 teaspoons lemon juice
2 tablespoons chopped parsley
for the saffron sauce
1 sachet saffron strands
4 tablespoons milk
6 oz (170 g) fromage blanc or quark
4 tablespoons plain yoghurt
1 tablespoon lemon juice
for the garnish
sprigs of chervil

Both sauce and filling may be made in advance. To make the sauce, shake the saffron into the milk in a cup, and stand in a small pan of simmering water for 10 minutes, to infuse. Allow to cool.

Put the fromage blanc and yoghurt into a blender or food processor, with the lemon juice and salt and pepper to taste. Process until blended, then add the saffron milk and process again. Set aside.

To make the filling, put the crabmeat into a bowl. Put the milk into a small saucepan with the onion, bay leaf, clove, salt, pepper and nutmeg. Bring to the boil slowly, then remove from the heat, cover and set aside for 10 minutes, to infuse. Then strain and reheat.

Melt the butter in a clean saucepan, blend in the flour, and cook for 1 minute. Gradually add the hot milk, stirring until smooth, and simmer for 3 minutes, stirring often.

Allow the sauce to cool, then mix in the crab, lemon juice and parsley. Check the seasoning.

About 1 hour before serving, heat the oven to 400°F (200°C, gas mark 6).

To make the pastry, sift the flour with the salt into a mixing bowl. Add the butter and rub in with the fingertips until the mixture resembles fine breadcrumbs. Add the lemon juice and 4-5 tablespoons iced water and mix to a soft dough. (Or the pastry may be made in a food processor.) Wrap in clingfilm and chill in the refrigerator for 20 minutes.

Roll out the pastry very thinly, about ⅛ in (3 mm) thick, then cut into 3-in (7.5-cm) circles, using the rim of a glass or a plain biscuit cutter. Roll each circle out again until about 3½ in (8.5 cm) wide. Lay 1 dessertspoon filling on one side of each circle, dampen the edges, and fold over to make a crescent. Press the edges together firmly to seal.

Lay the pasties on a greased baking sheet. Beat the egg yolk with the milk, and brush all over the pasties. Bake for 15 minutes until golden brown. Serve immediately, on warm plates, with a pool of saffron sauce on one side of each plate, decorated with a sprig of chervil.

Above: Tomato and Mustard Tarts (page 72).

Above: Small Cheese Pasties (page 73).

Above: Crab Pasties with Saffron Sauce.

Above: Leek and Mushroom Tarts (page 72).

TOMATO AND MUSTARD TARTS

Illustrated on page 71

These little tarts are quite quick to make and very delicious. They would be nice before a fish dish, or poultry, meat or game.

––––––––––– MAKES 6 –––––––––––

for the pastry
8 oz (225 g) plain flour
a pinch of salt
4 oz (120 g) chilled butter, diced
1 egg yolk
for the glaze
1 egg yolk
1 tablespoon milk
for the filling
1½ tablespoons Dijon mustard
4 eggs, beaten
¼ pint (150 ml) crème fraîche or double cream
¼ pint (150 ml) milk
salt and freshly ground black pepper
1 lb (450 g) tomatoes, skinned, seeded and chopped
2 oz (50 g) Gruyère cheese, grated

Heat the oven to 400°F (200°C, gas mark 6).

Sift the flour with the salt into a mixing bowl, add the butter and rub in with the fingertips until the mixture resembles fine breadcrumbs. Add the egg yolk and about 2-3 tablespoons iced water, just enough to mix to a dough. (Or the pastry may be made in a food processor.) Wrap in clingfilm and chill in the refrigerator for 20 minutes.

Roll out the pastry thinly and use to line 6 individual flan tins. Line with foil, weight down with beans and bake blind for 6 minutes. Remove the beans and foil, brush the pastry with the egg yolk beaten with the milk, and bake for a further 6 minutes. Remove from the oven and leave to cool.

Turn down the oven to 325°F (160°C, gas mark 3).

Shortly before serving, spread a thin layer of mustard in the bottom of each pastry case. Mix the eggs with the cream and milk, seasoning with salt and pepper to taste. Stir in the tomatoes with all but 2 tablespoons of the cheese, then spoon into the pastry cases. Sprinkle with the reserved cheese.

Bake for 20 minutes, until golden brown and slightly puffy. Serve immediately.

LEEK AND MUSHROOM TARTS

Illustrated on page 71

Small vegetable tarts, served hot, make a lovely first course, and could well be followed by a cold main dish, either fish or meat.

––––––––––– MAKES 6 –––––––––––

for the pastry
8 oz (225 g) plain flour
a pinch of salt
3 oz (85 g) Cheddar cheese, finely grated
3 oz (85 g) chilled butter, diced
for the glaze
1 egg yolk
1 tablespoon milk
for the filling
8 oz (225 g) mushrooms, caps only, chopped
2 oz (50 g) butter
1 large leek, white part only, chopped
1 tablespoon plain flour
5 tablespoons milk
salt and freshly ground black pepper
1 large egg, separated

To make the pastry, sift the flour with the salt into a mixing bowl, add the grated cheese and butter and rub in with the fingertips until the mixture resembles fine breadcrumbs. Add about 6 tablespoons iced water and mix until the dough forms a ball. (Or the pastry may be made in a food processor.) Wrap in clingfilm and chill in the refrigerator for 20 minutes.

Meanwhile, cook the mushrooms gently in half the butter until softened, then drain in a colander. Bring ½ pint (280 ml) very lightly salted water to the boil and add the leek; cook for 5 minutes, then drain, reserving the water. Return the water to the pan and boil until reduced to about 5 tablespoons, tasting to make sure it doesn't get too salty. Make up to ¼ pint (150 ml) with milk.

Heat the oven to 400°F (200°C, gas mark 6).

Roll out the pastry thinly and use to line 6 individual flan tins. Chill for a further 10 minutes, then line with foil, weight down with beans and bake blind for 6 minutes. Remove the beans and foil, brush the pastry with the egg yolk beaten with the milk, and bake for a further 6 minutes. Remove from the oven and leave to cool.

Melt the remaining butter in a saucepan, blend in the flour and cook for 1 minute, stirring. Gradually add the heated leek and milk mixture, stirring until smooth, then simmer for 3 minutes. Add the drained leeks and heat through, then remove from the heat and stir in the lightly beaten egg yolk. Leave to cool for a few moments.

Whisk the egg white stiffly, then fold into the leek mixture. Divide the chopped mushrooms between the pastry cases, then cover with the foamy leek mixture. Bake for 15-20 minutes, until puffy and golden brown. Serve immediately.

SMALL CHEESE PASTIES
Illustrated on page 71

These little cheese pasties may be served alone, with drinks before the meal, or as part of a mixed hors d'oeuvre. They could be accompanied by a dish of Caponata (page 32), Grilled Pepper and Tomato Salad (page 37), or a simple tomato salad and a plate of sliced prosciutto or salami. Most things could follow this: a beef casserole, or a chicken dish, or boiled beef with salsa verde.

MAKES 12

½ lb (225 g) filo pastry sheets
1½ oz (40 g) butter, melted
for the cheese filling
4 oz (120 g) cream cheese
3 oz (85 g) grated Parmesan cheese
1 egg, beaten
salt and freshly ground black pepper
1 tablespoon chopped mint

Heat the oven to 350°F (180°C, gas mark 4).

To make the filling, mash the cream cheese with a fork and mix in the Parmesan. Stir in the egg, then season with salt and pepper to taste. Mix until creamy, then stir in the mint.

Unwrap the filo pastry and remove 1 sheet. Roll up the remainder, and cover with a damp cloth so that it does not dry out and become brittle. Cut the filo sheet into strips about 10 in (25 cm) long and 3 in (7.5 cm) wide. Brush them lightly with melted butter. Lay a heaped teaspoon of filling at one end. Fold in the edges, about ½ in (1 cm) on each side, to partly enclose the filling, then roll up the strip so that the filling is totally enclosed. Brush all over with melted butter, press the edges to seal and lay on a baking sheet. Continue in the same way until all the filling is used up. Wrap the remaining filo and freeze for another occasion.

Bake the pasties for 15 minutes, or until golden-brown. Serve hot, soon after baking.

MUSHROOMS EN CROUTE

These crisp mushroom treats are quite filling; follow them with a light dish, possibly poached or grilled fish.

SERVES 6

2 small white loaves, 1-2 days old
2½ oz (75 g) butter, melted
1 large clove garlic, peeled
for the mushroom filling
2 lb (900 g) small mushrooms
8 shallots, finely chopped
6 tablespoons sunflower oil
4 tablespoons dry white vermouth
salt and freshly ground black pepper
1 tablespoon light soy sauce
3 tablespoons chopped parsley
3 tablespoons chopped chives

Heat the oven to 400°F (200°C, gas mark 6).

Melt the butter with the garlic clove and set aside for 10 minutes, to flavour the butter.

Cut each loaf crossways into 3 slices 2 in (5 cm) thick. Remove the crusts and trim each slice to a rectangle about 3×2½×2 in (7.5×6.5×5 cm). Using a small sharp knife and your fingers, remove the centre of each slice, leaving a case ¼ in (6 mm) thick.

Brush the bread cases all over, inside and out, with the garlic butter. Lay them on a baking sheet and bake for 8 minutes, until golden brown.

Wipe the mushrooms, discard the stalks and cut the caps into quarters. Heat the oil in a frying pan with a lid and fry the chopped shallots for 2 minutes, then add the mushrooms and cook briskly until all the oil is absorbed. Add the vermouth, with salt and pepper to taste, cover and cook gently for 5-6 minutes, until the mushrooms have softened. Stir in the soy sauce and half the herbs. Remove from the heat.

Place the croûtes on individual plates, and spoon the mushrooms with their juices in and around them. Sprinkle with the remaining chopped herbs, and serve.

Left: Mushrooms en Croûte, right:
Wholewheat Quiche with Herbs and Cheese (page 76).

WHOLEWHEAT QUICHE WITH HERBS AND CHEESE

Illustrated on page 74/75

This is quite filling, and needs only a light dish to follow, perhaps a fish salad.

--- SERVES 6 ---

for the pastry
4 oz (120 g) plain wholewheat flour
4 oz (120 g) plain white flour
1¼ teaspoons baking powder
a pinch of salt
4 oz (120 g) chilled butter, diced
2 teaspoons lemon juice
for the glaze
1 egg yolk
1½ tablespoons milk
for the filling
1½ lb (675 g) mixed green leaves in season – sorrel, spinach, chard, watercress, cos lettuce or parsley
8 oz (225 g) firm Brie
6 oz (170 g) ricotta or fromage blanc
6 tablespoons freshly grated Parmesan cheese
¼ pint (150 ml) single cream
3 eggs, lightly beaten
salt and freshly ground black pepper
4 tablespoons chopped dill

To make the pastry, combine the flours with the baking powder and salt in a mixing bowl. Add the butter and rub in with the fingertips until the mixture resembles fine breadcrumbs. Add the lemon juice and about 5 tablespoons iced water, just enough to mix to a dough. (Or the pastry may be made in a food processor.) Wrap in clingfilm and chill in the refrigerator for 20 minutes.

Heat the oven to 400°F (200°C, gas mark 6).

Roll out the pastry and use to line a 10-in (25-cm) flan tin. Line with foil and weight down with beans. Bake blind for 8 minutes. Remove the foil and beans, brush all over with the egg yolk beaten with the milk and bake for a further 6 minutes. Remove from the oven and cool.

Turn down the oven to 350°F (180°C, gas mark 4).

Bring a large saucepan of water to the boil and add all the green leaves (except the dill). Cook for 5 minutes, then drain. Cool slightly, then squeeze out the moisture and chop roughly into pieces ½ in (1 cm) square.

Cut the rind off the Brie, and chop it into small cubes, about ¼ in (6 mm). Put the ricotta into a blender or food processor with 4 tablespoons of the Parmesan and the cream. Process until blended, then add the beaten eggs and process again, very briefly.

Tip the mixture into a bowl and season to taste. Stir in the Brie and dill. Spread the chopped greens in the pastry case and pour over the cheese mixture. Sprinkle with the remaining Parmesan. Bake for 35-40 minutes, until the filling is set and lightly coloured. Serve.

CHEESE STRAWS

Illustrated on page 13

These make a good accompaniment to a clear vegetable soup or consommé; they are also good served with drinks.

--- MAKES 36 STRAWS ---

2 oz (50 g) plain flour
1 oz (25 g) chilled butter, diced
1½ oz (40 g) Parmesan cheese, freshly grated
1 egg yolk
½ teaspoon mustard powder
salt
cayenne pepper
butter for greasing

Heat the oven to 400°F (200°C, gas mark 6).

Sift the flour into a mixing bowl. Add the butter and rub in with the fingertips until the mixture resembles fine breadcrumbs. Add all but 1 tablespoon of the Parmesan and the mustard powder, with a pinch of salt and a pinch of cayenne. Stir to mix, then add the eggs with a very little iced water, just enough for the dough to form a ball. (Or the pastry may be made in the food processor.) Wrap in clingfilm and chill for 1 hour.

Roll the dough out until about ⅛ in (3 mm) thick. Cut into sticks about 3 in (7.5 cm) long and ¼ in (6 mm) wide. Lay them on a greased baking sheet and sprinkle with the reserved grated Parmesan. Bake for about 5 minutes, until golden-brown. Serve hot. They may be made in advance and reheated, but are best eaten the same day as made.

SAFFRON BREAD
Illustrated on page 7

This golden bread is an excellent accompaniment to fish soups, fish terrines or pâtés, or fish salads. It can also be dried, and used for croûtons with fish soup.

─────────── MAKES A 1 lb (480 g) LOAF ───────────

1 lb (450 g) white bread flour
1 teaspoon salt
½ oz (15 g) fresh yeast
¼ pint (150 ml) milk
2 sachets saffron powder
2 eggs, beaten
1 egg yolk, beaten
extra flour for dusting
vegetable oil for greasing

Put the flour and salt into a warmed mixing bowl. Put the yeast into a cup with 4 tablespoons tepid water and stand in a warm place for 10 minutes.

Put the milk into a small pan, add the saffron and heat until it just reaches boiling point, then immediately remove from the heat and leave to cool until blood heat.

Make a well in the flour and pour in the yeast mixture. Draw in the flour to cover, then add the saffron milk and

the 2 eggs. Mix well with a wooden spoon, adding a little extra milk if the mixture seems too dry. Turn the dough on to a floured board and knead for about 5 minutes. Wash out, dry and oil the mixing bowl. Return the dough to the bowl, cover with clingfilm and leave in a warm place for 1 hour.

Punch the dough down, turn on to a floured surface and knead again for 4-5 minutes. Then turn into an oiled 1½-lb (675-g) loaf tin and leave to rise for a further 45 minutes.

Heat the oven to 375°F (190°C, gas mark 5).

Brush the top of the loaf with egg yolk and bake for 30 minutes, or until the base of the loaf sounds hollow when tapped with the knuckles. Remove from the oven and transfer to a wire rack. Serve warm.

ONION BREAD
Illustrated on page 61

This is a delicious bread for serving with pâtés, with vegetable soups, or with vegetable dishes cooked in oil. It is best served warm, about 1 hour after baking.

─────────── MAKES A 1 lb (480 g) LOAF ───────────

1 lb (450 g) unbleached white bread flour
½ teaspoon salt
½ oz (15 g) fresh yeast
2 oz (50 g) butter
1 lb (450 g) onions, thinly sliced
2 egg yolks, beaten
salt and freshly ground black pepper
extra flour for dusting
vegetable oil for greasing

Put the flour into a warmed mixing bowl with ½ teaspoon salt. Put the yeast into a cup with 3 tablespoons warm water and stand in a warm place for 10 minutes, until frothy. Make a well in the centre of the flour and pour in the yeast mixture. Add ½ pint (280 ml) warm >

< water and mix with a wooden spoon until it starts to hold together.

Turn on to a floured board and knead briskly, sprinkling with more flour if necessary. Knead for 5 minutes. Wash out, dry and oil the mixing bowl, then return the dough to the bowl and cover with clingfilm. Stand in a warm place for 1½-2 hours, until doubled in volume.

Punch the dough down, turn on to a floured surface and knead again for a further 5 minutes. Form into a flat round shape and lay on a greased baking sheet sprinkled with flour. Return to a warm place to prove for a further 45 minutes.

Meanwhile, melt the butter in a frying pan with a lid, add the onions and cook gently, covered, until soft and very lightly coloured. Do not allow to brown. Season with salt and pepper.

Heat the oven to 450°F (230°C, gas mark 8).

Pile the onions on top of the loaf just before baking. Brush the onions and the sides of the loaf with the egg yolk. Bake for 15 minutes.

Turn down the oven to 425°F (220°C, gas mark 7) and bake for a further 30 minutes.

Check from time to time to make sure the onions don't over-brown; if they show signs of doing so, cover them loosely with a sheet of foil.

Remove from the oven and transfer to a wire rack. Serve warm, about 1 hour after taking out of the oven.

BREAD STICKS

Illustrated on page 64-65

Freshly baked bread sticks are a far cry from the grissini that are sold in packets and found in Italian restaurants. They are delicious served still warm from the oven, with soups, salads, and dishes of vegetables in oil.

--- MAKES 16 ---

¼ oz (8 g) fresh yeast
1½ teaspoons sugar
½ teaspoon salt
8 oz (225 g) white bread flour
1 tablespoon olive oil
1 egg, beaten
2-3 tablespoons sesame seeds

Put the yeast into a cup with the sugar and 3 tablespoons tepid water. Leave in a warm place for 10 minutes. Dissolve the salt in a little hot water, then make up to ¼ pint (150 ml) with warm water.

Put the flour into a warmed mixing bowl and make a well in the centre. Pour in the yeast mixture, followed by the oil. Draw in the flour to cover and stir in enough of the warm salty water to make it all cling together. Stir until well mixed, then turn on to a floured surface and knead for 3-4 minutes, until the dough feels smooth and elastic. Cover with a cloth and leave in a warm place for 5 minutes.

Heat the oven to 300°F (150°C, gas mark 2).

Knead the dough once or twice more, then divide it into 16 pieces, and shape into rolls about as thick as your middle finger. Lay on an oiled baking sheet and stand in a warm place for 12-15 minutes until they start to expand. Then brush them with the beaten egg, sprinkle with sesame seeds, and bake for about 35 minutes, until golden-brown. Cool on a wire rack for 10-15 minutes before serving to enjoy them at their best; alternatively they can be kept warm for a time, or reheated. But they must be eaten the same day as made. Otherwise, freeze them once they have cooled.

INDEX